Ideal America

Copyright ©2025 by John Benedict
All rights reserved

Printed in the United States of America
No part of this book may be used or reproduced
in any manner whatsoever without written permission
except in the case of brief quotations
embodied in articles or reviews.

ISBN:
979-8-9916874-4-7

Other books by John Benedict

Encyclopedia of the Abundant Life
What is a Democrat.

Soon to be published

War, Personification of Evil
Encyclopedia of Christian Action

Ideal America

by
John Bendict

Table of Contents

	Introduction	vii
	Prologue	ix
A.	Unity	1
B.	Patriotism	11
C.	Financial Management	15
D.	Taxes Must Match Expenditures	31
E.	Responsible and Disciplined Country	33
F.	Strengthen Political Leadership	35
G.	Change Election Laws	39
H.	Media Returns to 4th Estate Responsibility	47
I.	Courts Need to Be Apolitical	52
J.	Public Schools Not Performing	57
K.	Private Education Becomes the Norm	67
L.	Universities Focus Just on Education	76
M.	Health System Totally Changed	81
N.	Processed Foods	99

O.	Transportation Requires More Efficiency	101
P.	Laws Enforced	108
Q.	Crimes Greatly Reduced	112
R.	Caring for the Poor, Sick, Mentally Handicapped and Those Suffering from Natural Disasters	117
S.	Racism Needs a Soft Landing	121
T.	Encourage Religion	125
U.	Free Speech for All Not Just Protestors	127
V.	Immigration	129
W.	Government Wiser in Handling Crises	135
X.	Corporations Get Over the Greed	139
Y	Waste	152
Z	Youth	154
	A Final Word	159
	About the Author	163

Introduction

You might say that I have been in a front row seat to political history in America. My interest started in 1964 as a political student. Every day since then, often for at least an hour, I read, followed and participated in politics including attending state conventions and caucuses, even chairing in some cases. My focus also includes writing letters to newspaper editors in major cities and open discussions concerning the positive and negatives of politicians. I have intense knowledge about American politicians beginning with J. F. Kennedy. My book brings forth, and simplifies to some degree, what has transpired during that time period. To live the political system for over 60 years is much more than simply reading someone else's interpretation; it is to intimately and intuitively know 100 percent that my opinion counts and sheds light on our ever-evolving political system.

Prologue

I must confess up front that I voted for Lyndon Baines Johnson for President but have become conservative through the years and vote mostly for Republicans. But as this book will testify, I am dreaming about a country that would be contrary to what both parties are doing in many situations.

America is in a storm of problems and the first step toward solving a problem is to admit and state it. My judgment along with many that I know believes that America is corrupt, inefficient, and divided. I have a theory about corruption. Whether it is a country or a church, the entity starts off with excellent ideas based upon truth, honest intent and creativity but the longer it lasts the more corruption and violations of the original intent grows. Man has an element of selfishness and irresponsibility built into their character. But of course, as the country grew (immensely for America), the original founders eventually died off and the successors eventually were those who did not have the original intent and dedication in mind but were more intent on popularity, being elected and charity (means giving other people's money away for votes).

Andrew Johnson is a good example. He succeeded Lincoln on Lincoln's assassination. Lincoln embodied a principled leader and led the North through the Civil War. He also championed the principle in our constitution that all men are created equal, that they are endowed by their Creator with certain unalienable Rights, that among these are Life, Liberty and the pursuit of Happiness. The slaves were included in "all men". Now if Lincoln had not been assassinated, I have no doubt that the South would not have continued having slaves (paid slaves) for another 100 years but Johnson had no principles, no sense of justice, and did not even honor the 600,000 men that died because of Lincoln's principle. His lack of principle leadership prevented America of being free and honoring the constitution.

My dream is not just to return to the original America and upgrade the Revolutionary America to a mature one based upon our progress in population, complexity and problems but also reverse the downward trend in a way that would greatly change whole systems causing many people to change their participation in America. Citizens would have to change in their attitudes, expectations and discipline. Government would have to change to be responsible and to represent the people in a positive way that is good for Americans and for America. Government would have to stop adding burdens to some Americans and giving rewards to others. Americans have grown to expect many things that will disappear or change. Most Americans are unaware of a storm of heavy burdens that are arriving due to political choices that have been made. There is an impossible task of living as Americans are now. The top issues are debt on the one hand and losing the value of the dollar on the other.

Giving up the old ways may be hard but only for a time for following the suggestions in this book will give new life, a positive attitude about America and patriotism like we haven't seen for years, if not centuries.

Ideal America

The basic way of life in America will be different but different in a good way for America. We will no longer be on a downward slide. Debt will not loom as financial ruin. Social Security and Medicare will not be in danger of being unable to continue. Our health care and education systems will no longer be among the worst in the well-advanced world but improved dramatically. America will put its finances in a responsible and mature position. Medical and education will be affordable and efficient. America will be the country that I want it to be and I dare say many of you will feel that way too.

This book is really a dream about an America that would be productive, majestic, friendly, helpful and fair.

A.
Unity

What a great topic to start the dream for America!

If I had an organization that America should imitate, I would choose Alcoholics Anonymous. America has become a group of individuals like alcoholics who only try to satisfy themselves. They would like to have others join them but only to do what the alcoholic wanted to do. At AA, their situation changed. Everyone was an alcoholic and at AA they recognized they have their lost lives in common. The only way they can be redeemed was to join with others who were in the same place and support, help, join, and encourage each other. Each one needs a sponsor who is their fallback person, always there to lend a hand.

Amazingly, an alcoholic can't be 'here today and gone tomorrow.' He must come every day together with his brothers and sisters to grow, encourage and practice real life. When one believes in a Higher Power, one falls into the hands of God. First one recognizes there is a God and then to connect with God helps one live an unselfish life giving up the one thing for which they were living that brought only dependence and unhappiness. Now, they would be once again a part of God's family.

We are, after all, one big family. Families fight, I know, but families also work things out and do the best they can to make sure all members would be safe and healthy.

John Benedict

Is our American family united now? No! If we stay this way, we should change the name to the Divided States of America (DSA). How are we divided? Let me count the ways:

1. First of all, the division of our political parties are at an extreme never before seen. Never has politics in America been so divided. Congressmen vote against a proposal by the other Party, not for America but to keep the other Party from progress or admiration for doing the right thing because after all, America wasn't important, only the Party and getting elected the next time.

    We are so divided that a bill that is good for America will not be supported by the other Party because it will give them too much credit. The perfect example is the Infrastructure Bill to upgrade our transportation elements such as roads, rails, bridges etc. for a decade or more each Party brought tried to pass that bill when they were in power and the other Party would vote against it. Finally in the early 2020's the Republicans gave in and supported the Bill by the Democrats.

2. Protests are everywhere. I sometimes think that many people sit around trying to think of ways to be offended or upset about something. How many protests have we had in the last 5 years? Polls have estimated that between 15 million and 26 million people have participated at some point in negative demonstrations in the United States, making them the largest protests in United States history, maybe any country's history. But realize that is only 5%-8% of Americans. How can such

a minority receive so much media coverage? Could it be that our media is not working for America but looking to report on discontent and trouble?

3. What are examples of protests? Let us study the riots caused by the death of George Floyd in Minneapolis and how that impacted Minneapolis-St. Paul, Portland and many other large cities. The George Floyd incident was one large example of the uselessness and damage of a protest. Minneapolis was the center of the George Floyd protests. A crime alleged, (there are still some arguments against that.) by a Minneapolis policeman gave fodder to those who focused on the racial issue in America. A crime by a policeman was a terrible thing but with 700,000 policemen in this country, policemen cannot be totally crime free. A crime by a policeman would be extremely rare but inevitable. All policemen cannot be perfect.

4. Incredibly, there are professional protesters, people who are paid to protest and even given weapons and objects to throw at police officers or start fires with explosions. The new federal justice system is beginning to investigate these acts that have been ignored by the past administration, even though it has been obvious and even confessed in news interviews.

I must note that I wrote more details on this incident based upon a journalist who was dramatically affected by the event. Not only was she a reporter on this incident but her husband was a captain in the police. She wrote a book called *They're Lying* that paints a totally different picture than what the political leaders of Minnesota and the media presented.

John Benedict

A hundred minorities can be killed in Chicago in a single month and not receive any media attention. Three policemen can be ambushed in Houston, killed by minorities, but was nearly ignored by the media. But one incident in Minneapolis involving the murder of one man (who had been convicted of 8 crimes, spent 4 years in jail, and was stopped because the police were told by a store clerk that he had just used a counterfeit $20 bill), could become the focus of the media, keep racism alive and encourage other malcontents in America.

One crime in Minneapolis was taken by the news media and became the trigger of the most protests ever in this country. In fact, it became a worldwide story. Minneapolis nearly exploded with protests. Not only local protesters but protesters from around America participated. Many of the protesters were paid by wealthy agitators.

Protesting is a way of becoming public with a grievance that one can find and adopt to advance one's ego, enjoy vandalism without penalty or penance and receive headlines, maybe even an interview on national television.
What were the results of the riots?

- 164 buildings were destroyed by arson
- $500 million of property was lost
- 2 deaths just in Minneapolis
- Destroyed 350 businesses
- Destruction of a police precinct building
- The murder rate of blacks throughout America increased substantially, which is the opposite of what the protestors were seen as wanting

- Portland began 100 days of continuous riots causing much more damage
- Other cities in America had sympathy riots causing death and property damage
- Minneapolis and many other cities still suffer from this incident. They cut back on the police and many police took early retirement or a job with a city that supports the police. Result? Crime at record levels.

Look what was written about the protests in Portland on the same issue by The Atlantic: On the weeks before Labor Day 2020, Ted Wheeler, the mayor of Portland, Oregon, began warning people that he believed someone would soon be killed by extremists in his city. Portland was preparing for the 100th consecutive day of conflict among anti-police protesters, right-wing counter protesters, and the police themselves. Night after night, hundreds of people clashed in the streets. They attacked one another with baseball bats, Tasers, bear spray, fireworks. They filled balloons with urine and marbles and fired them with slingshots at police officers. The police lobbed flash-bang grenades. One man shot another in the eye with a paintball gun and pointed a loaded revolver at a screaming crowd. The FBI notified the public of a bomb threat against federal buildings in the city. Several homemade bombs were hurled into a group of people in a city park.

What is the latest protest?

We have protests here in America over the Gaza-Israeli war. That was happening in another continent and while it had a federal interest, we were finding states and city councils passing regulations about it. How absurd! Immigrants are inciting most of these riots and wealthy agitators are backing them. We don't want immigrants bringing their countries with them. If they don't want to be Americans, don't come. Nor do we want local politicians sticking their nose into business that does not come under their purview. Surely, they have enough to do without trying to solve a problem 7000 miles away totally out of their jurisdiction. In many of their districts, crime has mushroomed and their citizens are unsafe. Maybe they should spend some time on American problems. Or should we protest those local politicians for not doing their jobs costing citizens an unsafe environment and being biased against the Jewish race?

I saw a Palestinian protester interviewed and as you might expect, she had no idea what was going on in Israel. She happened to be gay and did not know that Palestinians have severe punishment for gay people, even death at times. She also had little, if any, knowledge about the attack on Israel innocents by Hamas. She obviously was just a professional protestor. Why should an insignificant person with no knowledge about the issue be allowed to upset progress, education, transportation and be shown by the negative media every day? Insignificant people like this person receive free advertisement. No wonder America is in trouble.

Something different was also happening with those Gaza-Israel protests. A new hazard had arisen for the protestors. 100 law firms have taken any student who was involved in the protests off their list of possible employees. They do not want agitators in their employ. That was a wise thing to do. Wealthy benefactors of universities were also withholding their money when colleges allowed this type of disruption on campus. The students were there to learn, rather than find some cause to disrupt the purpose of most students that were serious about their education. One billionaire requested Harvard release the names of the students involved in blaming Israel for the Hamas attacks. The names were eventually posted but not by Harvard.

The infamous Jan. 6 riot resulted in the arrest of 944 defendants and 562 have been sentenced to terms in jail and set the country in a divisive state once again because it was a political issue. The media has focused on this riot for nearly four years as if there wasn't something better and more positive to report. Why not report on education, debt, energy, and homelessness? Those topics were germane to this country and needed to be communicated constantly to voters. The Capitol riot was insignificant compared to the ones in Minneapolis and Portland. Are a few hours at our capital much bigger than months of damage and crowds of protestors burning down a police station and vandalizing federal buildings in Minneapolis, Portland and almost all the cities in America? All of this burning down and vandalizing tried to soothe someone's hate but apparently, that was not as important as the few hours at the capital. You don't suppose it had something to do with politics, do you??

What have these protests accomplished? Certainly not unity but greater division. Murders in our cities have gone up. Looting and other crimes have gone up too. The acrimony could very well erupt into small wars. Assassinations of many key people in our political system, justice system and even in the media would be a possibility.

We need to make it more difficult for protestors instead of bending over backward to make their protests easy.

Trump was impeached using a tainted paper article. This went on for over 4 years. Some notable Democrats were talking impeachment before he took office in January of 2016. Can we assume intent in that activity or maybe just very poor respect for the voter's choice? That portrays a sense of animosity that should not exist in our political system. Animosity, hate and disagreement makes unity impossible and could result in terrible actions by individuals who were not well-balanced. Trump has been the recipient of hate generated by the media that may have caused the assassination attempt made in July of 2024.

Democratic justice systems have indicted the former president 93 times for issues that are unprecedented. Most political crimes are victimless crimes unlike murders, rape, looting, and carjacking. Our political crimes are historic and common but never has such an execution of law been pursued like this. Political crimes are sometimes penalized but almost never taken to trial. We seldom even hear about them. Now, by coincidence, the indictments happened just before the election. The sudden search for justice was obviously a political activity. Many Americans will view the indictments as an odious political warfare that will further divide and penalize the future.

A true crime with the most victims, that I think tops them all was using an individual's position to do American favors for other countries. That has been done repeatedly by a certain Secretary of State and a VP (who became president). Reaching into the taxpayer's pocket and taking money to give to another country for which you receive personal benefit was about as bad as it could get. The country is receiving billions of taxpayer's money while the American criminal is receiving millions in American dollars. Certainly, stealing billions of dollars from our taxpayers is worse than being a woman's man at some time in your life, violating a woman's personhood which she never even reported 23 years ago or exaggerating your net worth to get a loan. Those crimes just affect the person and his family. A very small group. Bribery using America as the leverage affects all Americans.

An assassination attempt became reality with the attempt on Trump in July 2024. More and more judges and people in the justice system are requiring security to be present all the time. Even the chief justices are now requiring security on their homes. Some protestors are actually confronting judges and politicians at their homes and in restaurants, a real violation of judges and politician's freedom to live a life in a free America. Do the protestors think their free speech the only one that counts? Apparently. They live in their own little world of negativity and care not about what it does to America.

There are more lawsuits occurring in our public life than one can possibly imagine. Lawsuits are being brought against the president's "executive orders," government information that was kept private, damage done by governments including the police, and the media for printing false information, etc. - common place today. All of these items, although legal, point to a war that will never end costing the government billions of dollars. Notably the government loses many of these lawsuits suggesting that government was not running an honest and citizen-oriented system.

So, what do we do now? We need to talk unity and we do that first of all by recognizing that everyone cannot get their own way. We need to go back to a democratic method of agreement. Families work out problems because they know that if they do not deal with issues, they will no longer be a family. Like AA, we need to come together even when we would be resistant because of our grudges. We need to forget about the negatives and concentrate more on the positives…for America.

One obtains unity by working at unity. That means you air your differences, try to find a solution and if you don't get the resolution that you want, take it to the voters. Then we have to accept what the voters said just as we have to accept what a jury said. But we all must have a sense of family and a desire for unity instead of trying to find more accusations and use slanderous names for those with whom we disagree.

And unity starts with obeying the law. Why have laws if we don't obey and enforce them? The unlawful acts of protesters are costing America a great deal in money, property, crime, image, unity, police activity, and justice. Protesters who are interfering with other Americans should be arrested. Let's lock them up even if we have to build a square mile of walls to put them behind. Then America can live free and thrive together as we seek to do what will be best for America. We can then all enjoy free speech.

Especially, as a later chapter will note, free speech must be reinterpreted to not be a weapon against the free speech of others. Free speech of a minority must not cost students education time, worker's worker time, blockage of transportation and, of course, property damage and personal injury.

Unity begins by having a purpose for unity. Our purpose is not to find issues to exploit, argue or insist upon having 'my way' even though 'I am' a small minority. We have 330 million people in America and probably everyone has an opinion contrary to the majority. Can you imagine if all 330 million protested to get their way??

Our purpose continues to be unity now and forever. Instead of storms, we need sunshine.

B.
Patriotism

What a seldom used name in our society! Patriotism is the feeling of love, devotion, and a sense of attachment to a country or state. Note it puts country first. How often do you see this? I see it quite often among those who lived through WWII. Anywhere Americans have shed their blood for America you find patriotic people. I dare say it is unusual to see a person who risked their life for America to be involved in protests.

In a recent celebration of the Normandy landing, veterans in their 90's remembered the night before the invasion. They were caught up in emotions we could not imagine. They were going into a naked beach against bunkers, barbed wire, mines and machine gun placements that had been installed for years. Everyone knew that many would lose their lives and many more would be injured, some injuries changing their lives forever.

But in the younger generation, who have been untouched by war, you see many who want to protest. The wars and sacrifices that the older generations have made breeds unity, courage, patriotism. Today's soft life breeds discontent, separation and protests it seems. Young people especially, participate in protests. How often have you heard that, "it is amazing how smart my parents have become since I grew up." When we were young our confidence and perception of ourselves was highly exaggerated justifying the challenge of history, decisions by adults and maybe anything which we could enjoy protesting. But like so many things, you can't know them until you experience them. And as you grow older you make mistakes that you would never do again.

Countries are like that too. No person is perfect. No country is perfect. The most mistakes were made while we were young. At a young age we can't even define patriotism because we haven't shed blood for America or suffered personally for America. In the case of America, we are still making mistakes after 250 years and they are just as bad, if not worse than 200 years ago. We have many more mistakes now too, because we have a much more complicated society.

Some who live on criticism of America are trying to remove the Pledge of Allegiance, even the anthem, and tear down historic monuments that involved people very instrumental to our history as well as religious symbols and quotations. If you have a major problem with what the majority honors maybe you should move to Siberia or Venezuela and see how they operate. Destroying symbols and quotations is typically executed by a small minority who make a lot of useless noise instead of being helpful in making America better.

I was set back when I heard that Cuban who owns the Dallas Mavericks has removed the anthem form the beginning of the game. Here is a man who became a billionaire because of American opportunity and now he wants to show his disgust for America? A crusade is frequently started by some college professor who is looking for some reason to be offended. He has probably never served his country, just benefited from it. College professors often live in an irresponsible world having been given tenure and the freedom to almost teach anything they want to teach.

Ideal America

What would happen if we all were willing to carry America's message of freedom and liberty and one of our major reasons for our lives is to make America a special country that it once was. A common purpose for all Americans would be the wind to drive our ship through storms and rescue the wrecks along the way. A mind is a marvelous thing. Don't waste it on personal items such as sports, entertainment, phones, and Facebook. Personal items are temporary. Make your time productive for you and all Americans. Consider each day how you could help America be free of all the corruption and inefficiency that has developed over nearly 300 years. Give up wanting a free lunch. Pay your way. Earn your keep. We can expect an overhaul after 250 years. Let us all determine to do something about it. Treat the flag and the anthem as something personal and prophetic.

History has quotes from patriots that help us understand patriotism.

- One of our most patriotic Americans Nathan Hale said, when he was captured by the British in the Revolutionary war, "I only regret that I have but one life to lose for my country!"
- John F. Kennedy's inaugural speech said, "Ask not what your country can do for you – ask what you can do for your country."
- Daniel Webster, "I was born an American; I will live an American; I shall die an American!"
- Woodrow Wilson, "The way to be patriotic in America is not only to love America, but to love the duty that lies nearest to our hand, and to know that in performing it we are serving our country."

John Benedict

Patriotism is like a football team. Once you are part of it and you know the people and make sacrifices to help the team, the team and other players become as important as you. So become a part of it. This is your country and mine. Let's change the B's. Instead of beating up on it, build it. Let's 'rebuild the walls, install a new kitchen and make the living room bigger.'

The best way to end this section is to paraphrase the most patriotic song of all by Irving Berlin:

> *God bless America*
> *Land that I love...*
> *My home, sweet home.*

C.
Financial Management

Most failures are connected to the handling of money. Businesses go broke, people go bankrupt, homes have to be confiscated, people have to move into their cars or an outdoor tent, employees don't get paid, all because of bad financial management.

Except America cannot go broke, cannot go bankrupt, cannot live in outdoor tents. But the people who live in America will suffer grave consequences if our financial management doesn't improve dramatically. The suffering will be uneven because those with money (and there are many) will be able to withstand the crises. Those with meager income and no net worth will suffer far worse than any American has ever suffered.

China has many trillions of America's monies because of our greed and reticence to set limits on our corporations. Imagine America controlled by China. We'd have no Social Security or Medicare, our roads and bridges would be unsafe, sewage collection and water supply iffy and unsafe.

The two big issues today are debt and inflation. These issues do not seem to be understood by the voters so their votes do not cause changes.

Today we are seeing that debt and inflation are deadly. People are no longer able to pay their rent and millions are having to move out with no place to go. Groceries and fuel have inflated to the point where there is no money left for rent. Many items have doubled in price from 2021 to 2024.

Once inflation becomes significant, the correction is very difficult. The Federal Reserve raises interest rates to stop inflation but that increases rents, and reduces construction and investments by companies, slowing the economy. Reagan stopped the terrible inflation of Jimmy Carter's presidency but the economy slowed down significantly in the action required to counter that inflation. However, the process was done very well and Reagan ended with a vibrant and healthy economy. Also, during that era, we were not faced with the incredible debt that we now have.

What causes inflation?

- One factor is demand-pull inflation, when there is an increase in demand for goods and services but not enough of a corresponding increase in supply. In the short term, businesses can't scale their production up quickly enough to meet the demand. As a result, prices increase.

- Cost-Push Inflation is the case of not only an increase in demand but an increase in production costs for businesses.

- Devaluation occurs when a currency loses value in comparison to other currencies. This makes imports more expensive and can lead to inflation. For example, if the Euro increases in price, then we have to pay more for the large number of imports that Americans buy.

- Higher wages affect inflation. Although higher wages may sound like a good thing for workers, some economic experts believe there can be some consequences, particularly when it comes to raising the minimum wage for workers. In addition, when workers have more money, they increase the demand once again causing inflation.

From this list it is easy to understand that demand and supply must be steady with small fluctuations for inflation to be low. The pandemic caused inflation because people did not spend money but, in many cases, stayed home. Many stores closed.

Once the pandemic was over there was such a backlog of need that people spent far more than normal. Factories could not keep up so they raised prices to help pay the expansion and added costs. The drastic actions taken seemed justified but the actions taken caused significant problems. Small businesses went broke. Suicides, divorces and mental issues multiplied and the level of inflation created difficulties for millions of people. Education took a real beating too as you will see on the education chapters.

Finances affect our way of life and the inflation caused by the drastic action of government was not free. To say that government over reacted is to minimize what happened.

Another factor is that inflation begets inflation. Manufacturers and stores take advantage of the inflationary atmosphere to raise prices that they do not need to raise but since people are used to price increases and expect them, a good opportunity exists for the manufacturer. During inflationary times, increased prices do not diminish sales.

One word stands out in explaining inflation: balance. There must be a balance in supply and demand. There must be a balance in our currencies with other currencies and there must be a balance in debt, only a little is acceptable.

Debt is much more difficult to understand. When we spend more as a country than we receive as tax income, the difference turns into national debt. In 2009 our national debt was approximately $10 trillion. In 2024, just 15 years later it is exceeding $35 trillion. Imagine a country 250 years old that accumulated $10 trillion of debt in 250 years and that same country today has accumulated $25 trillion more debt in just 15 years. It is regrettable that debt is not the #1 topic of all Americans.

What does debt mean to America?

- Our budget in 2024 included an additional debt of nearly $1.7 trillion because we didn't have the money that we needed to pay for all the things in the budget. In 2023, we spent $6.1 trillion and our revenue was only $4.4 trillion. Our income could only cover 72% of the outlay. How irresponsible is it to budget a large deficit?

- By fall 2024, the revenue to date was $3.754 trillion, while outlays for the period were $5.022 trillion. Our income would only cover 75% of the outlay with only 3 months left. That means that we were only receiving 75% of the money we needed to pay our government expenditures, which makes the debt problem much worse.

- Project that for 12 more years (3 presidential terms) and if major changes aren't made, we will be adding $20 trillion more debt.

Ideal America

- Our debt in mid-2024 was $35 trillion, about $220,000 per voter. If you had to pay a mortgage of $220,000 at the current rate of 7% that would be $15,400 per year. The maximum income on which you pay F.I.C.A. taxes are about $168,000. The trend right now is that our debt will be $50 trillion in just 8.4 years, which is late 2043. Since 2009 we have averaged nearly $1.8 trillion of debt each year.
- America has to pay interest on that debt. Our interest on the existing debt om 2024 is just over $1 trillion. In the fiscal year 2024 just ended, the government spent $6.75 trillion. How does the interest affect our budget?
  » 20% was for social security, the interest is equal to 2/3rds of this humongous bill
  » 16% Medicare, the interest is equal to 81% of that bill
  » 14% national defense, the interest is equal to almost all
  » 13% health, the interest is equal to all of the bill
- Does reducing our expenses seem like a possibility? It is possible. Just some 'top of the head' thoughts –
  » raise taxes on Social Security by $200 billion (entirely possible by elevating the maximum income subject to FICA taxes and have a graduated tax into the millions),
  » eliminate the Department of Education $80 billion,
  » stop the invasion of the border (now costing us $150.5 billion),

» cut subsidies on such things as EV cars, which is near 2 billion,
» cut the student loan payments that Biden is forcing through by the back door,
» cut the fraud in Medicare about $300 billion,
» raise import taxes on products that are competing with our American manufacturers, $200 billion,
» cut federal bureaucratic excess employment $400 billion,
» we experienced over $500 billion of fraud on the pandemic relief payments and there must be more fraud that we don't know about, etc.
» We can save hundreds of billions by converting from public to private schools (see chapter on education) but most of those savings accrue to state and local government.

The miscellaneous numbers are adding up to near the deficit for this year's budget.

Ideal America would start with several broad financial guidelines as follows:

America must never spend more than we have. Never use debt to make life easier for some or provide a free lunch to gain a special interest vote while placing a mortgage on everyone's head. We need to do what people do when they are broke. Stop spending. Live within our means – change our way of living. Cut corners on every item.

- We have an enormous number of wasted spending problems that must be corrected. As noted later, we have thousands of empty federal buildings costing billions to maintain. We have excess money going into programs that are terribly overstaffed. For example, the VA program, when criticized is given more money. That is the way to stop the criticism I suppose. I visited one of 1320 VA health care facilities, 1138 outpatient sites plus administration facilities. I walked into the facility, told the lady at the front that I needed some help. She said she would get some. I sat and looked at the bullpen of 'workers' that I could see from the lobby while I waited. The bullpen looked like a scene out of the Sabbath meant to be a rest day. I have never seen such a lethargic group in my life. They all looked like they were just killing time. And by the way, the lady at the front desk never came back so I gave up and left.

- Our education community keeps getting more money and tests show a decline in education. See the chapter on education. Systems don't have to have money to improve. In fact, in some cases we can reduce the money and do a better job. Focus must be on method and execution instead of finding ways to use more money with no value added. Or is the money going for more pensions and staff? A private school system could save hundreds of billions.

Correct our finances related to Social Security and Health. First, federal finances, which have not been on a sustainable footing for 23 years, are approaching a death spiral. Second, the largest component of our budget, the FICA-funded programs of Old Age, Survivors and Disability Insurance (OAS&DI) and Medicare, each are specifically unsustainable, according to an article by Edward Lotterman titled Real World Economy, Pioneer Press, May 26, 2024.

Stop the surge of debt. Our debt situation will require sacrifices such as we have never made before. If we don't take major action on this very soon, serious consequences will plague America forever and end our leadership in the world. Our way of living will diminish since we will not be able to afford our present and comfortable lifestyle. Today, instead of hoping to minimize our excess spending over the budget, we are expecting $1-2 trillion added debt each year. Provide responsibility for everyone to contribute to the financing of America, if not with money, then with time and attention. We must be dedicated to supporting those in need but not give to those who just want a better lifestyle.

Prioritize expenditures. First would be the provision of safety for the citizens from crime including violet crime and scams of every sort attacking, in many cases, our elderly. Military and health would be a close second. Infrastructure, social services, and the elimination of addictive drugs, some of which are deadly, would need to be budgeted according to the funds available. Once the essentials are covered, we no longer spend money.

Provide rules on money connections with other countries. Do not have situations where our policies make other countries rich and America poor.

Tax fairly, which is a big challenge. Keep in mind the needs of those with little or no income. Still keep in mind that those who live beyond their means are not rewarded. America is first before individual luxury or free lunches.

Elect people in important financial positions who have a grasp of the total financial picture and how it impacts everyone's financial future.

A couple negative examples–in the early 1980s, Congressman Barney Frank was assigned to work closely with the Federal Housing Finance Agency (Fannie Mae and Freddie Mac), part of the US government that guarantees most of the mortgages made in the United States. Frank gave speeches that everything was fine. Fannie and Freddie were not fine and crashed causing a long-term recession and hardship for many Americans. Too many mortgages were given to buyers that were buying above their ability to pay. Many financial experts and even the president knew before it happened that we were soon going to be in a big mess but a neophyte congressman with no financial degree or experience was key in preventing a disaster many people saw coming. He blocked the president and others from fixing the problem and then it exploded.

The recession could have been avoided had the right action been taken on a timely basis. Result of having the wrong person in a key job? Recession.

Be alert to financial direction that will lead to recession or inflation. A bad financial move cost many Savings and Loans and many investors a great deal of money. 1000 Savings and Loans went broke due to several factors both worldwide and local in the early 1980s. A law was passed by Congress allowing investments to be made and the taxes delayed until profits occurred in the future or the investment was sold. That made the building industry blossom encouraging many investors. Involved in this investment were loans, many with Savings and Loan companies because the money had to be put up front for construction. The construction industry boomed but then corruption set in and bad investments were made. Opportunists took advantage of the law causing Congress and the president to stop the law.

Unfortunately, congress did not grandfather the change so that people could continue giving to the completion of their investment allowing a natural death to the law that encouraged investment. Result? Investors suddenly stopped the money flow to partially constructed investments, of which there were many so the construction loans that contractors used were no longer being paid to Savings and Loan Associations causing a horrendous hit on that industry and interrupting America's economy.

Look at the big picture and the potential danger of a major bill. Donald Trump was another example of taking the wrong financial route resulting in disaster. He promoted a tax cut bill believing that it would spur the economy. Then we were hit with a pandemic and Trump lost his election, allowing Biden to upset the hope that Trump had for profiting from the tax bill.

Biden, for spite or a difference of opinion, took the nation into a different direction, wasting the tax cut and turning it into debt. Under the tax bill and pandemic, Trump added almost $8 trillion of debt, a record for 4 years. Biden was following a presidency that had added a large sum of debt and instead of moderating expenditures he expanded spending. Biden has had a shopping spree in four years giving money to every special interest Party that he knew and wasting expenditures such as the billions of dollars taken by fraud from Pandemic money. He has been able to exceed Trump's debt in four years even though he did not have the high initial COVID cost that Trump had.

The question always to be asked, "is the money for the potential crisis or to capture votes?". Many politicians throw money at a crisis like COVID but also go over the line in who and how much. This generosity is all funded by additional debt. Borrowing more money after the large debt from President Trump has put this country into a very difficult financial position. Biden also did not monitor all the money he threw at the pandemic. Hundreds of billions were captured by criminals, mostly overseas using fraudulent tactics that an examination and monitoring of the money would easily have recognized.

Having three presidents in a row that took wrong financial steps have added 24 trillion dollars of debt and it isn't done yet. We are operating in a way today that creates enormous new debt, higher than ever and climbing at a record rate. Debt is now over 125% of GDP, a ridiculous number.

Our country is not sensitive to the debt. For example, promises are made during the campaigns promising money for this special interest group and that. Where is all this money originating? Unfortunately, in the last presidential campaign, one candidate promised financial freedom for everyone without identifying who is providing that financial freedom money.

One issue that we don't realize is the damage that can be done by one wrong presidential decision. A president in particular has impacts that no one else can have while only having a 4- or 8-year responsibility on the impact that their governance makes. Often, they are thinking big or not thinking at all and everyone suffers not just for today but most notably after they are gone. Debt is insidious and will totally change our financial future. Debt is easy to do but terribly difficult to pay back.

We are following the example of Argentinians that was led by Peron to satisfy the desires of all Argentinians and by doing so their financial capability was spent. An easy way to obtain votes is to provide a free lunch for as many people as possible. That is human nature to want a free lunch. My dad was a farmer and he always voted for the candidate that gave the most subsidies to farmers.

Peron was one of the first to do that to an extreme. He gained total power by spending and it was disastrous in the long run. They have since been one of the worse risks' countries for investments in the world. Venezuela did the same thing and look at them now.

Why must we change our system?

- Provide more protection for warning signs such as future debt. The financial issues above create a mortgage costing every voter $200,000 just in the last 15 years. The interest on that annually will be in the neighborhood of $10,000 a year per person. You can't find a crime that costly anywhere near that much.

- Requite total agreement with 2/3 majority required to spend beyond a specified amount.

- Spending beyond your income starts a suicide cycle that leads an entity to financial dependence. Spending normally includes not only the cost of the item but the overhead that continues and the overhead typically continues to increase. Today, this country is spending $1.38 for every dollar of income we receive. The debt is climbing at a rate that will eventually sink us.

- We are paying one trillion a year just for interest. That adds to our debt too. That interest will continue to be a larger part of our spending and could become as much as we spend for everything now in time. Spending beyond the clearly established needs often leads to being unable to afford spending on the essentials.

In one case, a president tried to spend us out of a recession and instead prolonged it. In another case, two presidents overreached on a pandemic crisis. It was so carelessly managed that as much as $400 billion was scammed mostly by people outside the country. Our government is incompetent in supervising our spending. There are criminal violations in almost every area and we do not pursue those violations encouraging others to occur. Our government is such an easy target.

In regard to trade deficits, this is an unrecognized way that countries obtain money. China joined the World Trade Organization in 2001. Since then, our trade deficit with China has grown so that in 2022 the trade deficit with China was $367 billion. That is basically money that goes out of our pockets and into China's. The total deficit just to China for the last 22 years is nearly 5 trillion dollars.

Many changes could be made, for example:

- Monitor the money sent for a specific purpose. Find the fraud and prosecute it to the fullest extent of the law.

- Eliminate tax credits for electric vehicles. Let the consumer choose to buy the EV because of the features rather than the subsidies.

- Cut the tax credits embedded in the Inflation Reduction Act.

- Revise the federal workers pay to coincide with private workers and make hiring, firing and transferring senior federal officials easier as well as relocating agencies.

- Reduce the cost of illegal immigration. Only provide benefits when they have a job and can live economically on their own. Give them one year to achieve that status.
- Raise the requirements for student loans to insure they will be responsible to repay.
- Replace public schools with private schools.
- Cut the holidays. Some holidays are just for government workers, schools, and banks. The rest of us see it only as a day when we get no mail, cannot go to the bank, the kids have to stay home and government offices are closed. Juneteenth is a new holiday that was probably established to obtain votes. I guess that less than 1% celebrate that holiday and that includes people who get the time off. Those work hours given away are paid by the taxpayer but not productive. So, we taxpayers pay for a select few to have a day off. How many of you feel good about that?

Other ideas affecting our expenditures are following:

Outside of attacks by other countries the primary cause of failure is due to mismanagement of finances. Argentina was a good example. Peron gained power by proving this principle, you can gain power by giving free lunches to the voters.

Taxing fairly is a judgment call with many different opinions. One example is Social Security (F.I.C.A. taxes). It does not seem fair that Social Security is paid by a percentage up to $140,000 maximum income which is FICA taxable. Income above $140,000 is not taxable.So, a person making $140,000 pays 7% ($9800) while a person making 1 million pays $9800 (.1%). A worse illustration is that someone making $50,000 pays $3500 (7%) while a millionaire pays $9800 (.1%). The person making $50,000 will likely spend $6000 a year on groceries. The FICA cost is equal to almost 60% of what he spends on the biggest necessity of his life. There needs to be a major adjustment in the F.I.C.A. tax formula. We don't expect the millionaire to pay $75000 per year for that would be $3,000,000 in 40 years but his input must be more than .1% since $7500 a year is a pittance to a millionaire. Through hard work and/or good fortune, the person earning very large sums needs to show their thankfulness by helping those not so fortunate.

Much of the money spent on education and medication is spent through the influence of lobbying groups. For example, the two largest lobbying groups are the teacher's union and pharmaceutical companies. This paves the way for more pay in the education community rather than better education and health. The focus on education should be on education rather than money. Learning to read is not necessarily a matter of money but of technique. I have read an article that a very large school district can't even agree on the method to teach reading. That school district has a very bad accomplishment in teaching reading. 60 years ago, the children in my school had no problem learning to read. Why is it different today?

We need to downsize what some people call 'the swamp.' Government's big problem is that they do not have a way of controlling growth as private industry does. Private industry must earn their group by producing more. Government only needs a vote in Congress or the invention of a bureaucrat. Our government efficiency has become so low that we may be spending twice of what we should. As outlined earlier, I walked into a VA field office and was taken aback by the lack of activity. I would guess they were overstaffed by 50%. Remember each employee not only takes a good salary home but he receives early retirement and could possibly make as much in retirement as he did in his job. Many can live 30 years after retiring.

As an example of mismanagement, government buildings not in use are out of sight. There may be 77,000 empty or underutilized government buildings across the country. Taxpayers own them, and even vacant, they're expensive. The Office of Management and Budget says these buildings could be costing taxpayers $1.7 billion a year.

D.
Taxes Must Match Expenditures

Sounds impossible? No doubt but we have no choice. Either lose our financial health or pay our way out.

How do we do this?

First the tax code should be rewritten. Over the years through good lobbying and politicians who have little financial acumen, rules and exceptions have crept into the law so that a private individual cannot prepare his tax unless it is very simple and the income is very small. A big industry has arisen just to handle our complicated tax rules, not only for most taxpayers who have deductions for medical, charity, small business, etc. but also for the big taxpayer that needs a complete tax advisor system, usually the year around, to plan and report on their taxes. The account team must find and address every loophole and even construct ways of reducing their client's tax. Why should we create a big industry just to interpret our tax laws?

Everyone should pay some tax, even if it just a dollar. We are family. Remember? I have never campaigned that the rich should pay more. According to the latest data, the top 1 percent of earners in America pay 40.1 percent of federal taxes; the bottom 90 percent pay 28.6 percent. That sounds very fair. On the one hand, that appears to answer the complaint that the rich don't pay enough taxes but there is enormous wealth in that 1%. A millionaire used to be a very wealthy person. Not anymore. Being a millionaire is pretty common. Of course, many non-millionaires retire with a pension and if they live for 25 years they will likely spend as much as 2 million dollars. The question becomes how do we tax pensioners? So even those who are not millionaires are especially in jeopardy. In their retirement, many pensioners should be treated as millionaires too.

It sounds so easy to tax corporations but the argument is that corporations just add the tax to the price of the product so ultimately the consumer pays all taxes. Still for corporations to pay zero tax seems unseemly. All corporations should pay at least a minimum tax. Of course, if Congress corrects the many loopholes in our tax system, probably all corporations would pay tax.

America can't find enough taxes to pay what we are spending; we have to cut spending until income equals expenses. It sounds hard but some believe that government is only 50% efficient meaning you could cut at least 25% of the cost of the federal government.

Our country is spending $1.38 for every dollar of taxed income. For a country to plan on a tax that only provides $1 for every $1.38 spent, one has to be considered a complete imbecile at math and a betrayer of every man, woman and child in America.

E.
Responsible and Disciplined Country

We have attempted to lessen responsibility for citizens. By lessening citizen's responsibility, we make citizens irresponsible.

This country was founded on responsibility. Imagine driving a wagon across half the country filled with mountains, rivers, prairie, wild animals, Indians, and who knows what else. That would take a great deal more planning than a trip to Disneyland. Then too, they had to start over from scratch when they arrived at their destination. Build a home, plant crops, raise a herd of animals, etc. Imagine packing for such a journey and new home as compared to packing today for a trip or a move. Not only did the pioneer have to pack for the trip but for the living space and new home in an undeveloped state.

Today Americans in many cases can't even be responsible to find a job or cut back on their lifestyle. They want government (with taxpayer money) to support their everyday activity regardless of production. It is a free lunch mentality.

Estonia handled the recession in 2009 a different way than this country. We tried to make it easy for everyone by spending money that we didn't have. They decided to gut it out and they recovered in a fraction of the time that we experienced. Often enduring pain for a short time is easier than a severe itch forever. We now are saddled with 10 trillion dollars of debt accumulated during the recession recovery. That will amount to an additional debt of over $50,000 per taxpayer. which continues to grow over time due to interest cost. A smart financial government would have immediately begun to pay off that debt once the economy had recovered. But not America. We added another 8 trillion in 4 years to set a record. Then the pandemic set in and once again we went on a spending spree. It is as if an American can't stand pain of any kind but they feel comfortable with an enduring itch that keeps getting worse.

Discipline is a characteristic that requires work and determination. Without discipline we avoid the tough work and fall into a trap of letting others determine who and what we are. It takes discipline to enforce our laws. It takes discipline to say no to people who want a free lunch. It takes discipline to protect America from trade deficits that provide cheaper goods but makes America poorer. It takes discipline to vote for someone who is first of all concerned about America when his opponent might be more likable. It takes discipline to stop spending when the budget is being exceeded.

F. Strengthen Political Leadership

Our politicians that are elected must work to make America better rather than interrupt that activity to gain more votes for the next election. Politicians now spend as much as 4 hours a day raising money for the next election campaign. We have made their task doubly hard since they have their political responsibilities, while also having to raise money.

Politicians need to have a focus on the issues that challenge America. Their job should be more about working together within their Party and with representatives in the other Party to resolve the problems that face America. Notice the word "with" is used instead of "against."

They need to change from Party first to America first. A good example of Party first and one that is hardly mentioned by the leftist media is Biden's draw down of the Strategic Petroleum Reserve, which he did to save his obvious dilemma with gas prices. The reserve is now at the lowest level since 1984. First of all, it made little difference and secondly, that reserve is untouchable since it is an emergency measure. This was purely a deception that was self-motivated and ignored the long-term needs of Americans. A recent and large illustration of Party first is the election and support of Biden. He has now, after public demonstration of his senility, stepped aside revealing that he was probably not competent when elected to be president and only now when his mental condition was so obvious that the Party took steps to replace him. This support of a person so very unqualified to run the country was an example of how he was chosen only because of name recognition and the ability to beat Donald Trump. The position of president is so challenging on energy, mental capability and management experience that Biden's choice was clearly a case of not putting America first.

We should put an age limit on presidents. 80 is just too old for the CEO job of the largest organization in the world. Sure, some candidates do quite well at 80 and Senator Byrd died in office at 92 years of age on June 29, 2010 but he was not active in his office. His staff did all the work. No one has the energy and mental acuity at 80 as those in their 60s even 70s. The energy required as President is enormous. Not only policy and direction of a very diverse and large government including the military but all of the time spent with foreign affairs, public appearances, and visits with dignitaries of other countries is way too much for anyone in their 80s. To be under 80 at the end of their term 4 years later they would have to be 75 on inaugural day: 75 plus 4 years equals 79.

A second and seldom mentioned requirement of a president is management experience. No job is less fitted to a pure politician, someone who is trying to sell instead of manage. America is indeed one of the toughest manager positions in the world and that requirement is never even mentioned. Management skills required are planning, strategy, direction of others, leadership, decisiveness, dependability, conflict resolution, constructive criticism, delegating tasks, integrity, and mentoring. Those are skills you don't just suddenly possess when you become president.

How do politicians improve their fight for America?

America's concerns are secondary with much of our government. Look at illegal immigration. Efforts have been made with every president to reform a broken system. Nothing will pass because both Party's have different goals in mind. It may be that the Democrats are plying for votes while Republicans are more intent on enforcing the law. So, the situation continues to get worse. In the meantime, we are spending as much as $150 billion per year because of the excessive illegal immigration.

Why is debt so seldom discussed? Why is the quality of education not mentioned? Why is the extraordinary cost of health not a highlight? Instead, we hear mostly about Trump's trials and Biden's age. Why is that? America should not be driven by media gossip!

The partisan politics has reached a never before extreme preventing Congress and the president from governing for America, rather they are governing for Party. Note the recent history. Review ratifications of nominations to the Supreme Court and Federal Reserve Board together with cabinet positions. Well into the 1990s the prevailing consensus was that as long as a president's choice for such a position was not grossly unfit, they should be confirmed. As late as 2005, John Roberts, nominated by Republican George W. Bush, was confirmed as chief justice by a 78-22 vote. As many Democrats voted for him as against. In 1987, Alan Greenspan, nominated by Republican Ronald Reagan to head the Fed, was confirmed 89-4. As late as 1997, Roger Ferguson and Ed Gramlich, Democrat Bill Clinton nominees to the Fed, were confirmed by voice vote with no nays heard. Now all such nominations are on or near strict party-line votes.

Many times, in the past, an important bill has been offered by two Congressmen, one a Democrat and one a Republican. That is how it should be.

I have heard from one Congressman, who wanted to vote with the other Party, but did not because he would suffer more competition in his primary, have to spend more money and time in that campaign to say nothing about receiving less attractive positions in Congress such as chairing committees. That smacks of Party First, America Second, not only by Congressmen but the people that are active in his Party back home. This means that many extreme Americans run our political system. Extreme political workers who are the ones selected for state and federal nomination conventions have become very partisan. A climate must be controlled that gives politicians the freedom to do what they think is right rather than what extremist in their Party wants them to do.

One problem that exists more so now than before is the extremist politicians in each Party. They are pushing an agenda that the media is happy to publish but doesn't have a chance of being approved even in their own Party. I appreciate the passion that an extremist has but that must be used with good judgement. To threaten the Speaker's position, for example, because he doesn't push your extreme item and respond to every news reporter just itching to find disconcerted elements is counterproductive and disruptive to the team effort of the Party and bad for America.

G.
Change the Election Laws

In the 2019 Gallup poll only 40% of Americans answered "yes" when asked if they had confidence in the honesty of elections, and 59% said "no." After the 2020 elections, I dare say the number of "yes" answers will be smaller.

What can we do to improve our election system? This system needs to be fair, honest, cost less and give people who know what is happening in government the right to vote. The many cases of fraud and the system that invites fraud needs to be eliminated.

- First of all, the campaign should not be more than 4 months long. Today it is nearing 2 years. As soon as an election is over, there is talk and preparation for the next election in two years. Does that result in better candidates? The answer is emphatically no. The only service that is provided with a 2-year election cycle is gossip for the media to publish. Unfortunately, with our four-year fixed terms making campaigns 4 months long would be nearly impossible unless America changed to a British format.

- Too much money in our campaigns is another big issue. This allows the extremely wealthy to participate in a dominating way far beyond the average citizen. Their influence should be no more than that of any average citizen. To repair that imbalance remains a mystery.

- As you watch the campaign rhetoric, one can see that campaigns are governed by   marketing and advertising. The point is to learn what will attract the voting public's vote. Politicians plan their campaign around the "promises" that will be the most popular regardless of whether they can make it happen. Much is made of "promises" during campaigns that are not kept. First of all, they are not promises. They are election statements meant to attract votes. Secondly, no politician can make anything happen without acceptance by the Senate, House and White House. Even the president is very limited in what he can do independent of the Senate and House. Politicians often forget to use the word "plan" instead of the word "will."

- During a debate, the 'contestants' should be arguing policy and not calling each other names. Wouldn't it be wonderful if they debated our health system or education? Now those are huge issues, much bigger than Biden's age and Trump's lifestyle. Maybe some creativity in policy! Maybe some new ideas.

- The most common fallacies are claims of success where there is failure. For example, we have just experienced some of the worse inflation and crime in history. Claims are being made that inflation and crime has been reduced. That reduction is made after the same President watched the inflation and crime soar under his watch. Politicians choose the worse point in their own term instead of the point that they had in the beginning of their term. As my dad used to say, "Figures don't lie but liars figure."

- The voters are ultimately responsible, for they too have selfish motives or they are plainly uninformed since the 4th estate has not done their duty. Many have no interest in policy, Congress and the White House on a daily or even weekly basis. There are many more responsible and fun things to do than keep watch on the people that are serving, holding them responsible for what they said in their campaign. A citizen's responsibility does not end with the vote. The voter must supervise what the people they hired are doing. For example, a parent shouldn't bring kids into the world and then ignore their behavior.

- Identification and a questionnaire should be required of each voter. I have used my ID several times in just a week to buy products or to see a doctor, get help from my bank, etc. But the Democrats have fought voter ID at every turn claiming IDs are racist and something poor people cannot obtain and would therefore not vote. That appears to be a fallacious reason to justify eliminating IDs and therefore allowing voter fraud to be easy. There is no reason why everyone cannot provide an ID when they vote. When some claim that it is too hard to get an ID, I would be glad to bet a chicken dinner that they have a cell phone. If not, there are more than enough people involved in the voting process to do the leg work to obtain an ID for everyone.

- A questionnaire should be used to qualify voters. We should not have people voting a particular way because their grandmother told them they were Democrats or Republicans 20 years ago. One should vote out of knowledge not tradition or likeability. Many voters don't even know who the VP is, what the issues are that greatly affects our security, what our debt has become and how significant debt is becoming to our country and ultimately our way of life. We will have to deal with that but even more so, our grandchildren's lives will be altered in a direct and personal way because of our debt. Why should voters be allowed to vote only because they dislike the other Party for reasons they can't even express or were significant 80 years ago but not now. I find many react to an argument with the other Party that if they lose the argument, they call their opponent a racist, then politics becomes emotional instead of issue-oriented. Incredibly I just heard racist used when churches were discussed, citing that churches are mostly white and therefore racist. That word should be expunged from our vocabulary. Like free speech, it is used wrong so many times, it has lost its true meaning.
- When candidates campaign, they should argue how to make America better rather than castigate the other Party. This includes a pledge to not spend more than you have.
- Never propose legislation that benefits individual special interest at the expense of others in America.

Ideal America

We are family and our focus should be on the whole family not one spoiled child or one outlaw in the family.

- There should be as much interaction between politicians of separate parties as between politicians within the same Party. Communication breeds agreement and understanding enabling Congress to negotiate a bill that is not perfect for either side but for America. Negotiation is a respectable and necessary art to make America better. No one should expect to have 100% of their own way. In my experience, I have thought of the ideal solution to a problem but when I shared it with a group, I found either I did not have the right solution or my solution needed some changes. A body is always better than one individual.

How is voter fraud made easy?

- By not enforcing the 1993 National Voter Registration Act that requires states to take reasonable steps to clean voter rolls between elections. Dirty voter rolls are an open invitation to voter fraud since anyone who knows there are out of date names on the rolls can assume the identity of that person in states where no ID is required and same day registration is allowed.

- Make the emergency practices introduced in 2020 during the pandemic permanent including ballot harvesting, mailing absentee ballots to individuals who did not request them, and allow all mail-in voting.

- Outlaw the need for a voter photo ID so anyone can assume they are the person whose name they are using. This also makes it easier for non-U.S. citizens to vote.

- Abolish the Electoral College.

Actions that need to be taken:

- The election process needs more policing. For example, Illinois has 15 jurisdictions that have more voter registrations than citizens of voting age. That is true in a number of states. Many voter rolls have not been cleaned. A watch dog system has used lawsuits that have been successful in cutting 4 million names from rolls in several states and there is much more to do. Names on the rolls of people who have died or moved is an open invitation for voter fraud.

- Police the voting process to make it difficult for fraud. How do politicians in our cities continue to be elected with the high rate of crime and poor education? The answer may be, in part, voter fraud. In many instances, Milwaukee and Cleveland along with Illinois mentioned above, have districts that receive more votes than the number of eligible voters in the district. When you consider that typical voter participation is about 70%, receiving 10% more votes than voters, then the fraud is 57% of the votes. Since large cities have nearly as much population as the rest of the state, that can turn the whole state. There are three encouragements for fraud – not requiring an ID when you vote, a very large number of voters not being taken off the rolls when they die or move and being able to register on voting day by just signing your name. These encouragements enable one to plan and execute fraudulent activity. It has been rumored that some voters get on a bus and go from precinct-to-precinct casting votes fraudulently. These two encouragements are the only reason the same people can vote multiple times, especially in those states that do not require prior registration. Some states such as Minnesota will fight to the death against a referendum to require voter ID and they did one time and won although America lost.

- A few billionaires are having an impact on American votes that is out of proportion. They, in some cases, want a big change in America and with their money are having an impact. One example is the Soros money that is setting up prosecutors in large cities that are changing the rules on execution of justice. I don't know what the answer is but something needs to be done to keep billionaires down to the same level as other Americans. Why should one person with enormous money have more influence than anyone else? In the case of Soros, he wasn't even an American until well into his 60's. He is a Hungarian trying to change America to look more like a Hungary he wanted it to be. Soros claims to be helping democracy but like so many organizations, they use the name of the item they are trying to kill in their own name. Soros isn't just attacking democracy in America but all over the world. He has associations with 243 papers around the world that he influences in their reporting. Many would say he is trying to kill democracy, just the opposite of what he advertises.

- Some method should be devised so that a check can be made on votes. After the vote some process should be used to check the votes to make sure they are one vote for one voter and the voter must be alive and live in that precinct. Maybe this is a good job for AI (artificial intelligence). That could take the human element out of it and maintain the privacy.

H.
Media Must Return to 4th Estate Responsibility

We need a media to be what it was designed to be, a non-partisan overseer of government. How else will the citizens evaluate their representatives!

The news media, like so many things, has changed dramatically in the last few decades. But it has digressed from its original intent, to be the unbiased reporting agency for citizens. The news media quite naturally concentrates on car wrecks, murders, alligators, celebrities, sensation, negatives, disasters, political weaponizing to name a few items. This means the media has become a political and somewhat entertaining form of gossip. Like so many things in American, the media has become corrupted and partisan losing much of its original intent. Below are the changes that should be made.

- The media was once called the 4th estate. Meaning there would be a Congress, President, judicial system and their overseer the media. The public needs a reporting agency to keep track of what their president, senator and congressman are doing. How else can they determine how to vote.

John Benedict

- We need the media to keep us up-to-date on major legislation and what our personal representative is doing, not just negative issues to turn people against someone when all the details are not included or not even available. The headlines every day are frequently on tragic or criminal behavior, reporting, which is not going to make America ideal.

- To learn about the activities and decisions of our elected leaders without the media requires a great deal more time than the average voter has.

- We need the media to not be tainted by their biases. How else can we produce public opinion that is accurate and identifies the heart of our country? Journalists seem to have a bias, especially in politics, and they can't help themselves from communicating by body language, a negative word or just focusing on negative stories.

- Selective journalism should be avoided. The media should be reporting consistently on all parties in the same comparative way. News media can look very honest and fair when you don't know the unbalance of their reporting. One time during the 2016 election, the Washington Post reported 5-10 negative articles on one candidate every day while they reported almost zero negative stories on the other candidate. This is the easiest way for the media to be biased and much of the public is unaware of the bias. When I realized a newspaper was so unbalanced, I cancelled my subscription but few will follow suit.

- One day I talked to a German visiting this country

and we discussed politics. He was very negative about Trump who was president at the time. I asked where he got his news. It was CNN. I went to the gym often and while I rode the bicycle I watched many TV screens, one of which was CNN. It seemed like every day during Trump's term, CNN had a columnist or noted person interviewed who spoke only negative things about Trump, many of which were not true or just plain opinion. CNN was obviously devoted to keep Trump from winning again. How can our voters vote intelligently when the media is so biased? I read news from many sources but I suspect most voters have only 1 or two sources.

- The black communities feedback on news media may hint why cities are full of crime alongside poor education but yet the same politicians continue to win the vote. Whites are 35% more satisfied with the news media than blacks. Blacks want more news on crime, the economy, education, government and politics. They receive an enormous amount of news on entertainment, pop culture and sports by contrast, none of which will make America ideal.

- One thing is certain. If you want to know the true picture of politics, you have to work for it. One source is not enough. Two sources are not enough.

Note the variety of readers, sources, and changes:

- Is there a name for a person who loves reading the newspaper? "Lectiophile," which simply means the love of reading.

- We now have new opinion stations. We know that CNN, MSNBC and FOX NEWS are opinion stations although they also pose as news stations. The news is always tainted on opinion stations. That is fine but should there even be mixed stations so people are getting tainted news thinking this is unbiased?

- Fifty-eight percent of adults aged 18-34, and more than 60% adults aged 35+, read a newspaper.

- Seventy percent of households with income above $100K are newspaper readers. 63 million adults access newspaper content on their smartphone or tablet. Total circulation figures show that weekday print circulation fell 13 percent in 2022, while Sunday print circulation fell 16 percent. That illustrates that the use of digital news is growing.

- Industry reports demonstrate that newspaper readership is robust, that newspapers reach the educated and affluent audience that advertisers are seeking.

- Reading newspapers online has become more common. No delivery is required. One can receive daily papers from all over the country.

- Television's arrival in the 1950s began the decline of newspapers as most people's source of daily news. But the explosion of the Internet in the 1990s increased the range of media choices available to the average reader while further cutting into newspaper's dominance as the source of news. No doubt our younger citizens rely on digital for their source of news.

- Mainly through their efforts in a few years, the readability of US newspapers went from the 6th to the 11th-grade level, where it remains today. Perhaps that is a symptom of our digression in the quality of education too.

- The two publications with the largest circulations, TV Guide (13 million) and Reader's Digest (12 million), are written at the 9th-grade level. See *https://www.google.com/search?client=firefox-b-1-d&q=newspapers+dominance+of+readers*

Concluding this topic, America must be aware of several things:

- News media is biased and one must always check political news to verify its truthfulness. No single media is totally unbiased.

- To know what your elected officials are doing requires a variety of sources and extra effort.

- The media is racist in the sense that they publish political news that is biased toward expanding the thought of racism.

- The news media is no longer the 4th estate of America intended to keep Americans advised of what their politicians are doing.

I.
Courts Need to be Apolitical

The Supreme Court is charged with ensuring the American people equal justice under the law and is the guardian and interpreter of the constitution. American's Supreme Court is unique. No other country has one like it. This means that the Supreme Court must interpret the meaning of a law, decide if the law is relevant to a given set of facts and rule on how the law should be applied.

Each justice must be selected by the President and approved by the Senate. That was not too difficult until Robert Bork was nominated in 1987 by President Ronald Reagan. Bork was a lawyer, judge and served as Solicitor General as well as a legal scholar. Because of his writings and history, his opinions were well known. The Democratic committee that recommends the nominee to the Senate fought his nomination wholeheartedly with Biden as its chairman. They were successful in stopping the nomination and set a precedent. Since then, nominating justices is a risky and argumentative thing to do; the candidate must answer questions very carefully but still the growing new element of America to find fault and protest constantly appears.

When Clarence Thomas was selected, Anita Hill testified that he had committed some sexual misconduct but she was the only one that claimed that to be the case. It was very important that Democrats not allow Republicans to put a black man on the Supreme Court for that would minimize their racists campaign strategy against Republicans. There was a big disturbance that the media loved but Clarence carried the day accusing the Democrats of racism against him. Using the loudest cry of the Democrats against the Republicans was something the Democrats could not allow to stand so Clarence Thomas was nominated.

Recently, our parties have become so divided that adding a Supreme Court judge is almost totally partisan. That carries over to the other judges appointed by the President. The two parties need to have a concern for fair and honest justice. Granted there are differences between the two parties but that difference should not be so political and extreme.

- The Supreme Court is responsible to protect the constitution, considering it to be the backbone of our nation. The temptation to change it on a political basis is to turn the Supreme Court into a political instrument.

- Both parties should meet and develop guidelines for selecting judges so that we have a common type of judge and the votes are not so wide apart. Granted some differences will remain but not to the extent that it is today. One party is trying to pack the court because it is one sided at 6-3. And where will that end? Of course, both parties have, at one time been dominate in the number of judges assigned to the Court.

In our judicial system, there is an extreme lack of uniformity. Some judges are called hangmen judges because they are severe in their judgments. Others are seen to be on the side of the criminal allowing them repeated arrests and light or no punishment. Being light on criminal punishment results in recidivism, a terrible cost to citizens. The same criminal repeats the same crime over and over costing the citizen money he can't afford to lose and often times injury and even life. One of the worse cases of repeat crime is abuse in a marriage or relationship. How many times have you read that a man committed a crime against the wife or girlfriend and was given a restriction on seeing or even being close to his wife or girlfriend? After this has happened a few times, one day, when he is still free to focus on his hate, he kills her. A known criminal is allowed to follow through on his criminal evil desire because a judge wants to be a nice guy.

Another way of looking at this is the difference between those who judge according to the exact letters of the Constitution and those who believe that culture changes negate the constitution allowing judgmental rulings that would be more acceptable to the public today. This frees judges to make a decision based upon his political views, his personal views or how he interprets the culture. That becomes dangerous because then we are out of control in our justice system.

The Roe vs. Wade ruling fell into the political category. The Supreme Court made their decision based upon what they supposed the people would like. The Constitution has nothing that relates to abortion so Blackman, the Supreme Court judge who wrote the opinion, argued outside of the Constitution. Judges must make judgments based upon the written definitions of the Constitution. From a technical standpoint the Constitution does not deal with abortion. The 1973 Supreme Court decided to play Congress and make this ruling without Constitutional guidance.

The Roe vs. Wade decision duplicates one of the most cited decisions in Supreme Court history, the Dred Scott ruling in 1857 making all states slave states. At that time the Supreme Court majority was from the South that believed in slavery. Although the North ignored the ruling, it took the Civil War 4 years to correct the ruling. It took Roe vs. Wade nearly 50 years for the 1973 ruling to be corrected. Many pro-abortionists complain about the Supreme Court doing the wrong thing by reversing Roe vs. Wade. The Supreme Court was merely correcting the erroneous decision of 1973 but still allowed States to govern abortion. Is it not right to allow each state to make their own decision on abortion? Otherwise, we would continue the unfair position that those who strongly oppose abortion have no rights.

There also seems to be a disparity in judgments, based upon race and wealth. We have all seen programs on TV or real ones where the criminal is found not guilty but the evidence and those who know him well are convinced that he is guilty. The famous football player O. J. Simpson falls in that category. He had multiple attorneys that must have cost him millions. Many believe that no one without Simpson's money could have been found innocent.

By contrast many people charged with a crime have no money and have to take a lawyer appointed by the court. That lawyer's experience could be very little and his ability could be almost negligible. His pay is not great or he would be working in a more lucrative position. Here the person charged is at a big disadvantage where his fate is out of his control and his representation is questionable. I suspect there are many cases of wrong judgements being made, not just for the person with no money but also for the person with much money.

The same thing is true in the Civil Court. Often the person with the most money wins. Certainly, it is also an advantage to have the money in hand.

Yes, the Civil Court has its issues too. Personally, on one occasion I sued a company for pay that they owed. I waited 4 years for it to be tried. When we went before the judge, he told us that he did not have time to hear the case and that we needed to settle it. We were able to settle it given that choice but later we read in the paper that that judge was an alcoholic and went from lunch to a bar. Delayed justice became no justice. This was not a situation where money was the issue but fair treatment addressing the situation was obviously about as bad as it gets.

How do we resolve the inequities of the justice system? I was taught as a child that America has the best justice system in the world. I have come to believe we are anything but the best. Money seems to be the biggest reason why judgements are questionable. Lack of it in some cases and too much in another. I would like to do something about it. Any suggestions? Also there needs to be more consistent judgment. We should not have one judge harsh with the judgment and sentencing and another judge lenient. Many times, they are miles apart. That is not fair to Americans.

J.
Public Schools Not Performing

The quality of public education has diminished, severely in the pandemic era but I have experienced mediocre education for decades with my family. Public schools spent $927 billion on K-12 public education in 2020-2021. Today it must be well over $1 trillion. See NCES.ED.gov.

- One of the most-reviewed studies regarding education around the world involved 470,000 fifteen-year-old students. Each student was administered tests in math, science, and reading similar to the SAT or ACT exams (standardized tests used for college admissions in the U.S.). These exam scores were later compiled to determine each country's average score for each of the three subjects. Based on this study, China received the highest scores, followed by Korea, Finland, Hong Kong, Singapore, Canada, New Zealand, Japan, Australia and the Netherlands. These are the top ten countries. America is ranked #31 according to one chart. That is not American to have such a poor education system. We never achieved what we have achieved by being #31. Our education system has not kept up with the culture and it might be the culture that encourages people to spend less time on education. We read often that our educational system has reduced the challenges of the course so that we can pass people who are not educated. What a way to fix a problem!!

- For example, China is a country with a dedication to education, many studying 6 days a week. The days are longer than for workers in industry. If students are having problems with a course their parents will pay a tutor to bring them up to an acceptable level and many want to move up by achieving a great deal in education.

- In the educational system, there are fundamental disagreements on how to teach reading. For example, years ago the Department of Education for the city of Minneapolis decided to experiment by assigning some of the minority students to a small private school operated by a black couple. The city advised them that these children were not fast learners and they could expect 2-3 years for them to learn to read. The teaching couple didn't believe that and had them reading in 3 months. I remember learning to read and it was very simple. It doesn't take a scientist to invent a method, just time and concentration. I suspect that math and writing fall in the same category. The method can be very simple. The teacher must be a good teacher of course and sufficient time must be allotted for students to learn. This illustrates that public education is misguided on many fronts and I suspect the many layers of administration and invented rules inhibit public education from being successful. By the way, I have not been able to identify that Minneapolis adapted in any way to the independent school teaching methods. Even now their record on reading is dismal.

There is a rule that if you give people money that they don't need they will find a way to spend it. Spending money is easy. Finding the money is hard although not for the present administration in Washington. Washington spends money whether we have it or not. There seems to be more comfort in just adding to the debt for a source of money. We have accumulated $24 trillion of additional debt in just 14 years. Using debt money seems to have become a habit. And why not? Voter's love receiving more money. That is called job security although it is killing America. Debt is too complicated for the free lunch public to understand. The disaster appears to be gradual but the last few years of rapid growth is frightening fast since now we seem to accept $1-2 trillion deficits every year and interest on the debt has become a major part of the budget.

- Everyone wants more money but money often is not the solution and might even exacerbate the situation. For example, sending money to education and the VA system is often not the solution because management does not appear to be competent to correct the problems or identify the solutions before the added money so they certainly aren't capable of using the new money wisely. Living in a failed system kills creativity and responsibility. It is common for a department to receive a budget and have considerable money left over at the end of the budget period. Afraid if they don't spend it the budget next year will be less, they find ways (not necessarily good ones) to spend it before the end of the budget year. The VA problem, as the education problem can be argued, is not a money problem but a bureaucratic and method problem. Schools often try to solve problems by spending money for higher pay, more staff, more buildings when the real solution is the method of teaching and the curriculum.

- Schools are indoctrinating our children. The risk that all kids face today is the potential to be indoctrinated in public schools by their teachers, teacher's aides, and administrators. That may be subtle although in college there are professors who are quite bold in expressing their political or moral beliefs and requiring the students to accept that opinion or suffer grade adjustments. Parents do not send their children nor do the taxpayers pay schools to form political and moral values in the student's lives. Yet it is blatant and I suppose happens because people who run colleges like to think college is a free-thinking institution and everyone, including professors, can do their own thing except, they want students to think the way the professors think. Control of student's minds is more important to them than successful education.

    The public is coming awake. Colleges are beginning to suffer from the public avoiding universities who are in the indoctrination business and benefactors no longer being tolerant of such antics. Just recently Emerson College who allowed, almost fostered the Palestinian protests, has seen a dramatic decline in enrollment for the year beginning Fall of 2024. They now have a major financial problem not only because of enrollment income but because donors are beginning to cut back. That is happening everywhere in different amounts.

- Education is uneven throughout America. For example, the difference in quality of education between the urban minorities and the suburban schools in Minneapolis is the greatest in America. An example is in Minnesota where reading efficiency averages 48% while the black, indigenous and Latino third grade students average 34%. Yet, a common state and school board governs the middle class and minority schools while the Federal Department of Education sets rules and monitors performance. Of what value is all of this administration when such disparity exists under their leadership?

- Schools seem to be designed more for the teaching profession than the students. Increased funding is disproportionately aimed at more pay and pensions for the education community while test scores decline. Teaching is the number one lobbying group in the States and Washington, DC. The state spending the most on education is New York at $24,000 per student per year. Utah spends the least at $7600. Yet New York is ranked 22 and Utah is ranked 10th according to Imed Bouchrika, PHD, Co-Founder and Chief Data Scientist of US News. (See educationdata.com)

This shreds the theory that money produces better education.

- What could a private school funded by government do with $600,000 for one class of 25 students in New York or even $190,000 in Utah. If they had $600,000, they could meet in the Taj Mahal.

- In 1978, Jimmy Carter created the Education Department with a starting budget of $12 billion per year. For 2025, the president submitted a budget of $82.4 billion. Almost a 700% increase since Jimmy Carter created the Department. Yet the performance of education continues to diminish. What has the Dept. of Education accomplished beyond spending money and adding to the employment of bureaucrats?

- Teachers applied pressure during the pandemic to not educate in the classroom. They were with children at an age where COVID was almost nonexistent. Flu among this age group was nearly as serious as COVID. Also, arrangements could have been made to protect the teachers in the class room environment. The quality of teaching all children effectively and uniformly through the internet is dubious, maybe impossible. Recently I read of the results of education that was revealed with national testing. The number of 8th graders who could not read to that level was astounding and depressing. What is more fundamental than reading? About 48% of Minnesota third-graders scored as "proficient" on standardized reading tests in 2023, down from 57% five years ago.

Some states such as Florida did not panic during the pandemic and were closed only for months. Their education was almost totally unaffected by the pandemic. Here is a number that will blow you away. It is estimated that global learning losses from COVID-19 could cost this generation of students close to $21 trillion in lifetime earnings per the Education Finance Watch (EFW), which is a collaborative effort among the World Bank (WB), the Global Education Monitoring (GEM) Report, and the UNESCO Institute of Statistics (UIS). The EFW aims to provide an annual analysis of trends, patterns, and issues in education financing around the world. How much of that is America's loss? Saving the teachers from a low risk COVID environment was pretty expensive. Right?

What would improve teacher performance and satisfaction?

- Even teachers are unhappy with public school education. I have never talked to a teacher who didn't have some criticism of what was happening. Teachers do a marvelous job in a difficult system that uses a template crafted by others that is not applicable in many cases. Rules and direction from above are often tainted, political and ill advised. Pay is essentially the same regardless of the quality of teaching.

- I believe that teachers would be much happier in a private education system where government pays a fixed amount to each school. Pay could be given more on quality than paying the best the same as the worst. Teachers would have more choices in teaching and could interact with the parents directly instead of through a government-controlled system with an abundance of bureaucrats.

- The problem is not the teachers but the education system or education community, those many bureaucrats that never come in contact with the student but set standards and rules for the students and administer the system from afar. A private system would have to address the needs and wants of the parents and the standards of reading, writing and arithmetic. Shouldn't that be what education is about? Satisfying the needs of the customer?

Electing school board members is difficult for conservative performance-based candidates. There are a few strikes against winning that seat.

- First the election is often during off years where presidential and senatorial candidates are elected. So, the turnout is low.

- The average person does not know anything about the candidates. Voters are much more knowledgeable and interested in the major players running for president and senator to name a few of the well-known contests. Few people fully know the candidates for school board

- In many cases electing a person for the education board, is often kidnapped by the teacher's union because the election for school boards is typically offering candidates that are unfamiliar to the vast majority of voters. I have seen conservatives voted to the board and once the education community realizes what that means, they apply as much money and effort as they have, which is considerable to vote that conservative off the school board at the next election.

A private school system would not be political but education driven.

Finally, our public education system lacks sufficient teaching on health and finances. Is anything more important than good health? Good nutrition, exercise and a positive attitude will add 10-15 years to your life. Every semester should have health and finance studies. There is much to learn.

Finances are crucial in our complicated world. It takes a system, discipline and goals to have a positive life as you age. The art of financial management is to live within your means rather than your desires and keep track of your finances. By saving 10% per paycheck and living within your means, one can live independent of Social Security to say nothing about the joy of being able to enjoy life as you age with vacations and to help those in need. The financial demands are much greater today in this credit card era than they were 50 years ago.

A recent letter to the editor of a national paper tells the story of an exception in education where the teacher, Dr. Dave Kimball taught personal finance in the general business course. At their 55th class reunion, it was apparent that the students took the course to heart. There were an unusual number of affluent students present and they all attested to the teacher's planning and retirement pensions education. Such teaching would, without doubt change America significantly from a country with no understanding of personal finance and who live a very paycheck to paycheck life to one of knowledge, comfort and success.

A math course could be designed around managing your finances. Instead of a course that students don't know why they need it, this math course could gain a great deal of practical interest.

Every semester should have finance studies. There is so much to teach. Financial education would not only help the individual but the country making a new voter understand the financial problems and successes of the federal and state government, causing more votes for financial experience by Congress and presidents. The average American might even understand what $36 trillion of debt means.

We do not need a Department of Education in our federal government. We do not need school boards, city or county education administration, state administration and all the created positions that continue to multiply. I wonder if we have a Federal Department of Education because it is much easier to lobby one large entity than hundreds of smaller ones. In many cases today the customer (parents in this case) has little or no say in the education format for their children.

Would not a single state entity be sufficient for setting guidelines, provide funding and supervising private education? Let private education construct the education options that parents want. So far, the bureaucratic approach has been a failure as compared to other affluent countries.

K.
Private Education Becomes the Norm

Private education would accomplish many things – more opportunity for the teachers, better choice and quality of education for the student and the elimination of the non-productive bureaucracy of the district, county, state and federal department of education, all at a significant reduction in cost. Education would still be funded by the government but not controlled by them. Parents would once again gain control of what education their children received.

- Because private enterprise needs to be competitive and efficient to exist, schools can be designed for the needs and wants of the parents and students. By contrast, public education does not depend upon parent selection of the school or even parent satisfaction. Private education success will depend upon parent's choice of schools. That gives parents much more control in contrast to the existing public education that is run by government entities. Private education would easily be held accountable by parents unlike the existing system of public education administration. Government employees are not necessarily connected or dependent upon education successes.

- A good example of designing for needs is the student who was not in touch with today's curriculum. I know of a student who was poor in school. He had an artistic bent. He lit up when there was an opportunity to express his artistic talent. After he graduated from high school, he became a marine. After the marines he went to an art school and received an education to further his career in art. He is a hard worker and is very successful in commercial art. Don't you think much of his education in public schools were wasted? A private school that focused on art would have been a joyful and an enlightening experience.

- There is no successful measurement that affects the governments bank account. If an educational system runs out of money government just adds more taxes to the citizens. Private enterprise is between two goal posts. First, they must be good enough to attract students. Secondly, they need to make enough money to stay in business. They do not have a source of never-ending money. As in all private enterprise they must be competitive and offer the customer what they want.

- How can private education not beat the average student cost today? See the cost comparisons of states in my chapter on public education. New York, the most expensive school system, spends $24,000 per child per year. Utah, the least expensive state, spends $7600 per child yet, Utah is rated #10 and New York #22 in quality of education according to US News. That means that a class of 25 students costs $600,000 in New York and $190,000 in Utah.

Such disparity would not exist with a private system. The existing school term is 9 months. Imagine how private education could offer more intensity in schools enabling graduation sooner.

- Per-pupil funding for choice programs, on average, are as little as one-third the cost of public schools per an article by Marty Lueken published July 17, 2024. Marty Lueken is Director of the Fiscal Research and Education Center at EdChoice, a 501 nonprofit, nonpartisan organization. That is what bureaucracy and design by people other than parents have created. The weight of our government's multiple systems overhead is much heavier than our education performance. In a public system, politics enters in and makes a mockery of financial management. Only the government could create such an expensive system.

- More than half of recent four-year college graduates, 52 percent, are underemployed a year after they graduate, according to a new report from Strada Institute for the Future of Work and the Burning Glass Institute. A decade after graduation, 45 percent of them still don't hold a job that requires a four-year degree per Feb 22, 2024 article.

- Private education would have government funded support that is the result of taxes selected through the normal democratic system that we have. Private education would be dependent on government budgets just like public education. But the administration to manage a private system primarily on a financial basis would be a small fraction of the existing overhead produced by government. The money paid to private education, like all expenditures are determined by politicians who run the government and they in turn depend upon voters.

- Private education has a slimmer system than public education. No hierarchy of local, city, state and federal bureaucrats controlling the everyday classrooms with the same lessons designed for everyone the same regardless of need, interest or desired results. No complicated array of people all voicing the best way to teach. Private enterprise can construct the lessons to suit the needs of the student and especially the parent. Costs are less.

- A private system would be competitive. To make the education system pay for itself, the performance must be acceptable to the parents or they can readily change schools. The schools are not mandatory based upon locality and transportation system. The better run schools would be more efficient and productive.

- States would not vary dramatically as New York and Utah do. A private system would have much closer costs for education saving some states enormous amounts of money.

- A private system could be designed to specialize. For example, a school could specialize in health, science, the arts, and other curricula that serves the needs instead of the system designed by the state and or federal government. One size does not fit all in education.

- Teachers could be paid more by the value that they provide and those who are not effective can be replaced.
- The education calendar year could vary to suit the needs of the parents.
- Pensions and benefits for the teachers would be similar. They could still have the freedom to unionize.

Looking at other countries, I have chosen a few others to compare their systems with what I propose:

- Finland has a state-run, municipality-run and private schools. To qualify for public funding, all schools must receive a license from the Ministry of Education and Culture and align with the national curriculum and educational standards. While education is generally free, some courses charge modest fees. A foreign language is an example of a course that might require an extra fee. Finland apparently pays all school costs with a few restrictions as mentioned before. This would give a parent total choice in selecting education for their child.
- In India, private schools are called independent schools, but since some private schools receive financial aid from the government, it can be an aided or an unaided school. So, in a strict sense, a private school is an unaided independent school. For the purpose of this definition, only receipt of financial aid is considered, not land purchased from the government at a subsidized rate. It is within the power of both the union government and the state governments

to govern schools since Education appears in the Concurrent list of legislative subjects in the constitution. The practice has been for the union government to provide the broad policy directions while the states create their own rules and regulations for the administration of the sector. Among other things, this has also resulted in 30 different Examination Boards or academic authorities that conduct examinations for school leaving certificates. Legally, only non-profit trusts and societies can run schools in India. They will have to satisfy a number of infrastructure and human resource related criteria to get Recognition (a form of license) from the government. Critics of this system point out that this leads to corruption by school inspectors who check compliance and to fewer schools in a country that has the largest adult illiterate population in the world.

- In Germany Substitute Schools are ordinary primary or secondary schools, which are run by private individuals, private organizations or religious groups. These schools offer the same types of diplomas as public schools. Substitute Schools lack the freedom to operate completely outside government regulation. Teachers at Substitute Schools n must have at least the same education and at least the same wages as teachers at public schools, an Substitute Schools must have at least the same academic standards as a public school. Therefore, most Substitute Schools have very low tuition fees or offer scholarships, compared to most other Western European countries.

- There are secondary or post-secondary (non-tertiary) schools, which are run by private individuals, private organizations or rarely, religious groups, and offer a type of education, which is not available at public schools. Most of these schools are vocational schools. However, these vocational schools are not part of the German dual education system. They have the freedom to operate outside government regulation and are funded in whole by charging their students tuition fees.

- Northern Ireland, the internationally recognized definition of "private school" is misleading and a more accurate distinction is between fee-charging schools and non-fee-charging schools. This is because approximately 85% of all schools are private schools by virtue of not being owned by the state. The Roman Catholic Church is the largest owner of schools in Ireland, with other religious institutions owning the remaining private schools. Nevertheless, despite the vast majority of schools being under the ownership of private institutions, a large majority of all their costs, including teachers' salaries, are paid for by the Irish state. Of these private schools, only a very small minority actually charge fees.

    In 2007, The number of schools permitted to charge fees represents 7.6% of the 723 post primary level schools and they cater for 7.1% of the total enrolment. If a fee-charging school wishes to employ extra teachers they are paid for with school fees, which tend to be relatively low in Ireland compared to the rest of the world. Because state funding plays a fundamental role in the finances of all but one fee-charging school, they must undergo similar state inspection to non-fee-charging schools. This is due to the requirement that the state ensure that children receive a certain minimum education; Irish state subsidized fee-charging schools must still work towards the Junior Certificate and the Leaving Certificate, for example.

- In the Netherlands over two-thirds of state-funded schools operate autonomously, with many of these schools being linked to faith groups. The Program for International Student Assessment, coordinated by the OECD, ranks the education in the Netherlands as the 9th best in the world as of 2008, being significantly higher than the OECD average.

Summarizing the countries education system for the top educational countries listed above:

- Most countries provide state funded education for private or public schools.
- Faith based schools are dominant in the Netherlands and Northern Ireland with education being paid by the state.
- In most cases, the state determines the specifics on education. Note the state not the country sets that standard.
- In Germany the private schools offer education mostly vocational that is not available in public schools.

- Choice seems to be the general options at these countries so the parent can select the education for the child.

My recommendations are similar to many of the countries that far outperform us and are tilted toward private education. America's public system is so bureaucratic and expensive there are huge difficulties seen in eliminating public school education.

How would a private system be implemented? Unlike the ObamaCare system, one could use a trial system. Maybe choose a state or a city and rural area. The thought occurs to me that a bill to provide funding for both public and private schools in America would give parents a choice and cause a transition to private schools. Competition for public schools would cause a major rebirth of public education or it would die itself. The important issue for America is that the parents can choose the education for their child.

That would greatly minimize the risk but the quickest and easiest way might just be a law funding a fixed amount to all schools whether public or private. Then the parents would have a choice, the epitome of a democracy and in an American way the best way would be chosen.

L.
Universities Focus Just on Education

Colleges and universities have become too big and diversified to accomplish their mission of education. They are spending billions often on other items that are not education focused, preventing many from attending college for lack of money. This was inevitable since university expenditures keep rising, many times beyond inflation. Universities like other organizations keep expanding their activities beyond their primary task.

In contrast they are money machines through endowments, money given to them for investment for producing income. Many colleges and universities in the United States maintain a financial endowment consisting of assets such as financial securities and real estate. These assets generate returns that fund operational expenses. These endowments are enormous. Harvard that leads the way has an endowment of $52 billion. That is a considerable piggy bank.

Yet college tuition keeps rising, often more than inflation making college too expensive for many, who choose student loans. Many graduates are unable to pay their loans because they received a degree that produced a low paying job, failed to graduate or chose to live a life style that they cannot afford. That problem has attempted to be cured by using taxpayer money to pay loans, a totally unacceptable notion since many graduates have paid their way or worked their way through college. If education is paid by the taxpayer for some then all should be paid! Student loans total $1.6 trillion. With a debt of 36 trillion already America can certainly not afford free college tuition.

Instead of using the endowment for education, universities wonder into many activities that are not truly educational preparing our young people for careers. Instead, they are focused on many other items such as sports, hospitals, libraries, hundreds of extracurricular activities including drama theatre, for everyone, hobbies, community music programs, employment outside of the university, choreography, special interest societies, clubs on a variety of curricula but also on social justice.

If the focus was education predominantly, education would be more efficient and affordable. If each entity budgeted only for education, would education be much more affordable? I don't know the answer but I suspect it would make a major difference in the cost of education.

Why should universities not have different divisions, each of which supports themselves. Education would be first. That is a university's primary responsibility. Sports is typically a self-supporting entity. Hospitals are self-supporting and helpful for teaching medicine. Many divisions are not self-supporting. They certainly shouldn't be university supported.

Universities have many goals that are not profitable for students and make education more difficult. Universities stray into politics and changing societal norms evident especially in their support of protests and minority supported extremes.

In our universities, social justice is being taught with calls to action, which is clearly an invitation, almost a command for students to protest. For example, one student was accepted into a university because of a record of protest in high school! Some college applications ask students to describe their relationships with social justice, their leadership experience and their pet causes all to encourage protests and agitation in the university experience. Universities should not be involved in promoting social justice issues whether directly or indirectly. They are not Karl Marx but educators.

Professors are hired to teach not advertise their governmental ideas. Benefactors and parents should not be overridden by some professor's unique or defective ideas. Professors seeking to train their students into his political or moral thinking should be severely punished even to the extent of removing his tenure.

What could be worse for America than teaching discord and interrupting the free speech of others with a discordant "free speech"?

The loud protests and disruptions on campus over someone's grievances are occurring frequently, costing the universities acceptance and cutting back on contributions from alums. Some employers are crossing out those who protest from their recruiting list.

Universities have become cities with diverse interests and expenses. The expansion of university activities is often non-profitable and pulls the whole institution down.

An interesting measurement of this expansion is seen in their employment. The total employment at the University of Minnesota is about 27,000 max. with a student population of almost 55,000. That is about one employee for every two students. The result is very high tuition making it more and more difficult for people to obtain a degree. I don't know what employees of universities are paid but apparently too much for what they are producing. Salaries should be examined to justify the value received. Or maybe the outlandish ratio is due to universities spending so much time on non-educational issues.

Many students enroll in college to find a career. An interesting dilemma is happening. Many graduates can't find a job because their major just doesn't pay well. For example, if you took at African history, religious history, hospitality or fine arts, where do you get a job and at what salary? Enrollment had gone down 8% in the last year because of the job problem and the high cost to go to college.

Seeking a career by enrolling into college is a very expensive method. I graduated from engineering college and still had no idea what an engineer does when I graduated, having lived on a farm. Spending $35,000 to $50,000 per year at a university is certainly not a practical way to find a career. What happens when you graduate, find a job and the job is not what you want to do? Much of your education is then wasted. Colleges are not a good place to find a career. Most professors have never had a career outside of teaching so they are not a good resource.

Finding a career is much more practical by finding a job before you attend college. Then you experience work, a good way to find work that fits. Work is different than education. Colleges are not meant to find a career for students. It happens but only coincidentally. The better way is to find a job first which often lets you know what opportunities are available and what you would like to do. That gives you the best of both worlds. You are paid to find a career instead of paying a university to find you a career and you obtain work experience at the same time. Right now, blue collar jobs are the quickest way to employment. Blue collar workers are in great demand and earning more than many college graduates.

John Benedict

Education is beginning to find ways to make college more affordable. One major way is to cut the mandatory classes that have nothing to do with your major. For example, if one is seeking an engineering degree, of what value is psychology or even English. We all agree that education can ultimately be of value but where does that thought end. Could we not spend our entire lives becoming educated? By being focused on a degree, one should be able to graduate in 3 years instead of 4, which could reduce one's cost by 25% and apply you to the work force earlier and help employers fill empty slots. Of course, it would present a problem for universities since their income would be less and with an already bloated budget, financial problems will be significant.

President Trump's role in the White House is having an impact on the inefficient and distorted work of many parts of higher education. He has not encouraged and supported that distorted work. Trump has penalized universities for allowing, even encouraging antisemitism and disruption of education to be allowed on campus. Much of taxpayer's money is being channeled to universities for grants and to cover administrative costs. Because of the inefficient and distorted work of higher education, Trump is taking away funding for projects and tother funds that the universities receive from government. Universities are beginning to realize the serious blow that their non-education efforts cause, all a part of the bureaucratic waste that permeates so much of our government.

Universities have evolved into a mishmash of activity that has made education too expensive and interrupted by the university's perspective of societal justice, even supporting antisemitic activity. Let us return to education as our sole focus.

M.
Our Health System Totally Changed

Why do many believe our health care system is so overpriced, overused and not meeting the needs of the people? Read the following problems with America's health care system.

Cost is out of control. In 2022, U.S. healthcare cost was $4.5 trillion, which averages out to $13,493 per person (man, woman and child) per year. In 2010 it was $2.6 trillion. That is a 73% increase in just 12 years. The 2022 cost per person is double that of other wealthy countries. Although America is paying 50% more for medical per person than the second highest country, the longevity of Americans rates about 26th in the world. Longevity is perhaps the most important statistic to measure the effectiveness of health care. 50% higher is an extraordinary waste of money much of it being soaked up into a complicated out-of-control system of doctors, hospitals, labs, pharmaceuticals, and insurance companies.

The paper work under the present system is so great that the staffs, hired just to handle the reports, seem to rival the staff that cares for the patient. Studies found that half of the time doctors are not in front of the patient but reviewing tests, documenting patient visits, dealing with insurance, which has major tangles and snafus. Insurance alone can require an unbelievable amount of time and effort to have an MRI or a sleep study approved, never mind replace a broken CPAP machine. Then there are school physicals, letters of medical necessity, and disability forms. There is no end to the paperwork. One of the results of the Obamacare bill is more paperwork. It seems that every doctor's office and hospital have an abundance of people keeping records and handling the finances.

Are we healthier? No. Less healthy? Yes, and at a much greater cost. Note in a recent hospital visit of 3 days by a family member the bill was $150,000 and a list of the charges were not even available without extra effort on the part of the patient. If one argued with the charges, it wouldn't matter. You have no contract with the hospital enabling you to challenge their charges. Note this stay did not include surgery.

On a personal note, we were impressed with all the doctors that visited with my friend until I realized that each one must have taken a cut even though their visit was not requested or required. That and the enormous cost for medications, aspirin, and test add up to a big number.

Health care is a difficult item for buyers. Health usually is seen as the highest priority item and understanding the technology and making judgement on health care is very difficult for almost everyone. The consumer is at a big disadvantage to evaluate the treatment or even question the treatment.

PRECAUTIONARY TEST AND MEDICATION

In the $150,000 hospital just mentioned, the hospital chose to do a test that cost $13,500 even though it just took minutes. That was necessary in emergency since the family member had fallen and hit the back of her head. After three days in the trauma center, she was allowed to leave the hospital but the medical system ran the same $13,500 test again as a precautionary measure without explanation or asking for permission. I was not someone who could do anything about it although I didn't know until after the test.

It would be entirely ignorant of protocol to arbitrarily run a second test for $13,500 without explaining or even asking permission. Most people think long and hard before they buy a $13,500 product. But then insurance comes into play here since they can charge the insurance putting the doctor in control. This means that the patient is not in control. Neither is the insurance company. Once again no one is consistently in control, or you might say, control varies depending upon the situation. Without control, we realize the obvious gouging and excessive treatment.

Another way for the medical system to make money is in precautionary medicine. The doctor or hospital makes the decision and often without discussing it with the patient. As described above in the hospital example of $150,000 for 3 days, a second $13,500 test was run just before the patient was released from the hospital without discussing the test with the patient. One can buy a good car for $13,500.

Also, medications were prescribed that were precautionary. Precautionary medicine and tests sound good except that doing this with all patients raises insurance rates a great deal and now all insured patients pay more every year for ever. Precautionary tests and medications are arbitrary and a great amount of money is made by using care labeled as precautionary. Precautionary medicine has some justifiable instances but as with most of our medical system, the doctor may not be concerned about the money or he might be wanting to make more money with precautionary treatment.

How necessary are precautionary medicines? How frequently do you need this precaution? Is there a less expensive alternative?

How easy is it for a doctor to prescribe any number of precautionary medicines? Do doctors consider the cost at all?

INSURANCE AND WHO IS IN CONTROL OF PRICING

I need to state that insurance isn't free. Insurance just spreads the charges to everyone, which has an advantage except that there is no control of the amount of premium. Premiums are calculated to make the insurance company wealthy and are an accumulation of all medical charges including, doctors, nurses, hospitals, lab work, testing, medication and services. No one can keep track of this but insurance companies and they can then calculate how much to pay these bills and make a hefty profit.

There are two main problems with America's health care system;

First, patients don't have a choice most of the time and really no one single entity in the plethora of the medical system does. The doctor doesn't necessarily have a choice on what the insurance pays for a procedure. The hospital doesn't either and even the insurance company has limited control. The person who has the least choice is the patient. We have no choice in the system we use. America only has one system and that is not American to work without competition or choice.

Secondly, no one entity is in control. The five major parts of the medical system – government, doctors, labs, hospitals and insurance all work off each other to derive a pricing system. Each entity helps the other's increase prices. For example, Medicare has the most control of any but only pertains to a portion of the population. If a price is terribly wrong, how is it corrected? How does Medicare maintain its authority? Insurance is also involved in the pricing for various treatments. But no one entity is in charge so no one entity can be blamed for a high price.

America's system is based primarily on insurance. Insurance has become mandatory to protect people from the extremely high cost of sometimes simple medical procedures. Customers think of medical insurance as they do rent. It is a necessary expense. If you use logic, you realize that insurance has a large hand in increasing our medical cost. Health care in 2022 costs $4.465 trillion. Private insurance companies were over $1.4 trillion in 2022. When we pay premiums, we are also paying for the overhead and profit of each private health insurance company. That rivals the cost just for physician services. The disadvantage to the consumer is a loss of cost control. The advantage to the medical system is that price increases can be handled without involvement by the consumer. The consumer just ignores the high medical cost because their premiums rise but not as overwhelming as a large medical expense such as $150,000 for 3 days in the hospital or a $13,500 test that otherwise could pay for rent for a year. That gives the medical industry a free pass.

Insurance merely allows raises in the cost of medical by spreading the increases in medical cost over all those who are insured. Insurance cost protection is a deception by allowing all medical services to raise prices without the consumer knowing. Insurance premiums continue to increase so the consumer looks at the insurance company as the problem when they are merely cloaking health system raises. Of course, the insurance company not only enables higher medical cost, but adds the insurance company's overhead and profits to our medical cost. Because of insurance, the medical system has an easier way to raise prices as do labs and pharmaceuticals. No one has total control.

Insurance companies, on the one hand, control insurance payment for each type of procedure and yet can adjust the premiums if the costs rise. Yet they have to pay what other members of the medical team agree to price. That team includes doctors, hospitals, pharmaceutical and labs that run blood tests, do MRI's, etc. Although ownership is often different, they feed off each other.

Our system is one of those unique situations where everyone who benefits from higher prices has a hand in the pricing except the consumer. The consumer is left holding the bag (money) so to speak. The consumer ultimately pays if not in medical costs in premiums.

Doctors are the ones that are in the best position to control cost and treatment. But they are like any private business. They want to make as much profit as they can. They deserve good profits after taking so much education and then spending long hours working. But a major problem is that patients have little understanding of the technology and biology of medicine so they are not in a position to question charges or even choose what is best in their analysis and treatment. That means that the technology is too complicated for the consumer to evaluate the services.

BIG MONEY FOR LITTLE ITEMS

One way that doctors make money is with rules that require extra doctor visits. For example, to fill a prescription after a stated length of time, requires a doctor visit, which is charged at the going rate for a visit. They normally include the blood pressure, oxygen, and update to your records. The doctor visit is very short, he says a few words and orders a refill. The cost of the prescription then is typically multiplied by anywhere from 5 to 10 times when including the doctor visit. Granted there are some prescriptions that require a doctor's visit but very few.

As an example, I have had an itch for 10 years and occasionally run out of a big tub of salve that I use. My itch comes and goes. Recently the itch persisted and I was out of the salve. I couldn't get an appointment for 18 days for various reasons, none of them mine. The prescription was a no brainer for the doctor and also provided the doctor with an additional visit income of several hundred dollars.

Another recent example is a friend who broke her ankle and had severe contusions on her other ankle. She too, had to go through her primary doctor to see an orthopedic. It took 2 days to find an opening with the primary doctor and another two days to meet with the orthopedic. The primary doctor did absolutely nothing but sign off. No doubt many millions are made every year using this rule to expand profitability for doctors. Now in the case of nebulous rules the visit should be discounted dramatically. Why isn't it? Because consumers have no choice in our extremely expensive medical system. Money is all in the favor of the medical system.

MEDICATIONS

Medications have dominated the medical world. Most doctor visits end with a prescription. Yet, our longevity is poor. When I tell nurses that I take no medication they almost gasp. It is apparently quite rare. Providing a prescription instead of instructing a lifestyle that has a lasting impact on their health without drugs greatly reduces the time for the doctor with the patient. Less time per patient allows the doctor to see and bill more patients. But unfortunately, the patient is not better off, having now to face higher costs, potential after-effects and sometimes a continued medication crutch. This also might be substituted for a diet change or an exercise that would permanently cure the problem.

Medications dominate treatment of almost all health problems. 131 million people use 7 trillion prescriptions in America every year. The average number of prescriptions per person per year is 13. For those in the age of 65-79 the number is 27.3. With America leading the world in the use of pharmaceutical products, we rank 26th for longevity! Those points are contrary to each other and describe a major problem for America. Does this mean we spend this vast fortune on a product that may be causing us to die earlier.

There are 50 major pharmaceutical companies. America dominates the pharmaceutical industry with 56.1% of world sales. Europe is 2nd with 34.35% and Asia is third with only 9.6%. As with the manufacturing Americans use much more medication than other countries. Why? Good question. The advertising is incessant in America. Recently, TV advertisements have increased to the point where it is common to see 3-5 drug advertisements during one TV break. The medical professions and consumers have been sold on medication solving many problems. Many doctors fill their periodic license training requirements with pharmaceutical training. Pharmaceutical products overwhelm the medical industry with contact and technical information. There are as few as 10 doctors for each pharmaceutical sales person. Pharmaceuticals are a very profitable business since they can afford so much for sales effort. They also spend enormous amounts on lobbying efforts. Only the teacher's union spends more.

There are many stories of excessive care, which should be policed by the government. The most obvious one is polypharmacy wherein a patient can be taking 15-20 pills a day or more. This is very common. Hopkins, Mayo and other such notable institutions have studied polypharmacy and find it to be excessive and bad for the patient. It will frequently put the patient into never-never land so that they lose their mental acuity. No one controls that issue enabling pharmacies to make enormous profits over treatment that is damaging to the patient. Why don't doctors control that problem? I don't know. The only choice the consumer has is to take the list of medications, sit down with a pharmacist and obtain some technical information. A pharmacist might be their best resource for identifying the impact polypharmacy is having on the patient. They should know what prescriptions are duplicating, of no value, and which ones are interfering with others.

Another practice that is excessive is the quantity of a prescription, which seems to be written for the maximum length of time to cure the patient. In my experience one feels better right away wasting a substantial portion of the pills. The larger the prescription the more the cost so that helps the profitability of the pharmaceutical industry. I suspect the doctor prescribes what the pharmaceutical company recommends and they certainly would not recommend a minimum or even a medium dose.

One of the worse stories that I have heard regarding pharmaceuticals is the one where an acquaintance had 1 week left to live. The doctor approached the husband and said there was an experimental drug that they could try but no guarantees and the husband would have to agree. He did agree and his wife suffered the worse pain ever before she died in one week. Later they billed the husband $40,000 for the pill. Then we learned (and don't know if this occurred with this case) that it is common for a pharmaceutical company to pay the doctor as much as $500,000 to find a patient that would be the first test for a new medication on a human.

Testing is a source of revenue and that too is excessive. I have on two occasions met with a doctor and mentioned an issue that was not serious but made me curious. Instead of discussing the issue the doctor immediately suggested some test that would have been expensive. I knew it wasn't worth the test but I was surprised the doctor went immediately to testing.

URGENT CARE

One point that isn't very well-known or advertised is the urgent care route. Should we use doctors to handle the flu bug? Urgent care should be used much more than it is. I wonder how many doctor calls are better fit to the urgent care department. Each doctor should have an urgent care department or one next door. Why spend $400 for a cold?

CONSUMERS SHOULD SHARE THE BLAME

Let us not forget the consumers. They have adapted to the medical system in America and even become addicted to it. They overuse it and look for medication and doctor visits to take care of the problems that occur for lack of good nutrition and exercise. They also short change the idea that we were made with a miracle body and in most cases, it will heal itself if we give it some rest and care. Consumers want the fastest and easiest way out.

FRAUD

Another instance. My friend was an occupational therapist so she often worked in rehab and nursing homes. Management of nursing homes would dictate group treatment but bill Medicare for single treatment. Single treatment is much more effective as you can imagine. It was cheating but hard to monitor and enforce.

Many reports are available pointing to great fraud in Medicare. A couple examples: I was treated for an itch and early in my discussion with the doctor, I complained about waiting 18 days for a visit for an itch, which drove me nuts. She was offended and ended the visit so I received no treatment. But they still billed me for the visit. I did not pay the bill. But they did bill Medicare although no treatment was given. There was no one to protect Medicare. I have had, on a couple occasions, a doctor charge me an enormous fee until he learned that I was on Medicare and then he charged less so Medicare limits charges but I suspect that savings is made up in higher charges for medical services not covered by Medicare.

WHAT IS THE ANSWER

A mixture of government controlled universal health care for all and a private health care for those who choose it. Many will argue that putting government in control of health will eliminate the opportunity for private business and that is true but the private system today is doubling our cost of medical care and providing no longevity improvements. Someone has to be in control and it cannot be one profiting for their medical services.

Why not give the consumers a choice allowing private health to still be available. Without a government sponsored and paid alternative, no change can be made in our medical system. No one likes to have the government in charge but in this case, there is no alternative. The government is already controlling Medicare in a mixture of private and public control.

Even though there are estimates that Medicare cost is 20% fraud, the cost of Medicare compared to other private medical is much less because the government has an element of control. Without Medicare, there are 4 medical entities that act as a team to enrich each other. When evaluating universal health care, people point to Medicare, which saves seniors enormous amounts of money.

Government is the only one that can assume the authority to pay only what is justified therefore eliminating the insurance factor, which in many ways eliminates a key element in the team that together elevates prices without the consumers involvement.

No other entity has the unquestioned authority to manage medical care. Government does not have a profit motive so they can protect the consumer who is able to vote for politicians to affect the management. That is why, in this instance, only government-controlled payment of medical cost is the solution. Feeble attempts have been made to reform the medical system but it just becomes a political game and we lose.

When universal care is mentioned, the private sector screams and uses the tired argument that a person in Canada had to wait a year for surgery. To that story let me give you a few stories about America. In America, 60 % of surgeries are not needed; those dying in hospitals because of hospitals errors number 44,000 to 96,000 patients every year; every day in America, 750 older adults are hospitalized due to side effects from one or more medications; a simple visit to emergency can generate a bill of $5000; we rate 26th in longevity among all the affluent countries while being almost double in cost of the second most expensive country; spending a million dollars on cancer treatment while dying anyway is common. Don't you think America's stories are much more compelling than the tired story of the Canadian. Note: Canada may not be the best example of universal care. See the examples below of universal care that place countries far above that of America.

Imagine if we paid the government what we pay for insurance premiums. No doubt we would save money having government in control of medical costs. Then the voter would have some control over medical costs for the first time.

Here are examples of the best medical health care systems in the world: Four of the top health care systems in the world are Sweden, Belgium, Japan and Taiwan. Australia is included too because some references list them as 3rd. These five exhibit common features: Public funding of health care is included in all five of the references best medical systems which are managed by the government with private care options offered in some countries.

- Belgium's health care system is affordable and accessible. The country's health coverage covers almost the entire population with its wide scope of services and is a system publicly funded through Social Security and taxes. "Emphasizing preventative care, the system focuses on early detection and cost-effective measures," noted Insider Monkey. The country also, "boasts a strong network of health care providers and renowned medical research institutions like the University of Antwerp, Hasselt University and KU Leuven, among others."

  Belgium spends a significant amount on health care. The country is, "among the top ten spenders on health across EU countries, reaching 10.7% of GDP in 2019. With relatively high public spending on health, households' out-of-pocket payments amounted to 18.2%, spent mainly on non-reimbursed services, official co-payments and extra billings," noted a report by the European Health Observatory. Life expectancy is 84 for women and 80 for men.

- Japan has, "maintained a health insurance system that all permanent residents of Japan for more than three months are required to join, allowing people living in Japan to access appropriate health care services at a cost they can afford," noted the World Economic Forum. In addition, patients are allowed to, "choose any health care provider, from small clinics to large hospitals with the latest medical facilities, and all medical services are provided at a uniform price anywhere in Japan." The system is mostly publicly funded through taxpayer dollars, with some aspects of the system requiring self-pay or coinsurance.

The health care system, "covers 98.3% of the population, while the separate Public Social Assistance Program, for impoverished people, covers the remaining," noted Columbia University. The country has some of the best medical outcomes in the world, with the life expectancy at 88 for women and 82 for men. Infant and maternal mortality is also some of the lowest globally. The biggest risk to the system is the country's increasing medical costs caused by the "rapid aging of the population and sluggish income growth caused by slow economic growth," noted the World Economic Forum.

- Sweden's health care system is decentralized, or "nationally regulated and locally administered," where the "Ministry of Health and Social Affairs sets overall health policy," and the country's "regions finance and deliver health care services and the municipalities are responsible for the elderly and disabled," said the Commonwealth Fund. All legal residents automatically have health care. "There are both public and private providers of health care, and the same regulations apply to both," noted Sweden's website.

"The Swedish health care system has high public funding, universal coverage, an ambitious uptake of modern technologies and efforts to prevent unhealthy lifestyles," said the European Health Observatory. The life expectancy is approximately 85 for women and 82 for men, and maternal and infant mortality rates are low. "These attributes contribute to low levels of unmet needs, favorable health outcomes and good health status in the population compared with other countries."

- Taiwan has a universal health care system. "The single-payer system is funded primarily through payroll-based premiums, although the government provides generous premium subsidies for low-income households, civil servants and others," noted the Commonwealth Fund. "Health care services are provided mostly by contracted private providers." Every citizen and resident who has lived in the country for more than six months is required to be enrolled in the health care system.

    The country's single-payer system has been quite successful following decades of unsuccessful health care systems. "The benefits are quite comprehensive: hospital care, primary care, prescription drugs, traditional Chinese medicine," said Vox. "Patients must make copays when they visit the doctor or fill a prescription or go to the ER, but they are generally low." Life expectancy is 84 for women and 78 for men, and infant and maternal mortality rates are low. But hospitals are understaffed and overfilled because, "Taiwan's national health insurance has given patients such a good deal on medical care that they are overwhelming the system."

- Australia has an excellent, safe and affordable health care system, rated #3 in the world. Their system is much less expensive than America's. It is quite simple. They have both a private and a public system. Everyone can use the public system that is covered by a 1 ½ % tax paid by all taxpayers. If one chooses something that is not available from the public system or not from one's favorite doctor or hospital, one can use a private system buying insurance as we do in the States. This way the consumer has a choice, which is an American feature, or used to be.

Medicare has been Australia's universal health care scheme since 1984. Its 3 major parts are: 1. medical services 2. public hospitals 3. medicines. Many Australians have private health insurance coverage. Primary health networks (PHNs) are organizations that coordinate health services in local areas. There are 31 PHNs across Australia. The Australian, state and territory, and local governments share responsibility for running Australian health system.

So, what do we do? If America used some form of public and private system as these 5 countries have done, no doubt the cost would diminish a great deal and also most important, the consumer would have a choice to take the public system or invest in a private system. Note all five of these countries have longevity far above that of America. Australia ranks third in the world and Japan is one point better.

THE FUTURE LOOKS CHALLENGING

As you look in the beginning of this section at the growth in medical cost just since 2010, do you believe that the parabolic increase (if we stay with the present system) will continue in the future? I certainly do. Why do many who visit America return to their country for serious health issues? For example, many Germans who spend 6 months a year in America go home for health care. They describe the German health care as much less expensive and just as good or better than America's.

The high cost of medical care in the U.S. is one of the greatest challenges the country faces and it affects everything from the economy to individual behavior, according to an essay in the May-June 2020 issue of Harvard Magazine written by David Cutler, professor in the Department of Global Health and Population at Harvard T.H. Chan School of Public Health. Cutler explored key driving forces behind high health care costs—administrative expenses, corporate greed, price gouging, and higher utilization of costly medical technology.

In just a few decades our cost of healthcare has increased from 5% of GDP to 17% in 2022. Does anyone think this parabolic rise in health care cost will level out? If so, may I compliment you on your imagination?

AN EXCEPTIONAL PART OF OUR HEALTH SYSTEM

I need to put in a word for the best buy of the medical system that is seldom even mentioned. That would be the specialist, especially Physical Therapists and Occupational Therapists. They do not use drugs but use innovation and physical therapy (exercises, massage etc.) to treat. When people can't walk, have joints that hurt, pain in their limbs or back the first thing they do is go to a doctor. Too often the doctor writes a prescription to kill the pain. PT's know why they have the pain and introduce physical therapy to correct muscle issues, nerve issues, and program the patient to work at minimizing the problem. It is common for people to reluctantly go to a PT and leave with a smile and a new lease on life. The technology is much more challenging to know than it appears. Our muscles interact in a way no one can know without knowing the body's mechanics. For example, moving your hands is possible because of some muscles in your forearm.

As an example, an elderly lady checked into a physical therapy clinic because she could not move her head. She had seen doctors and was convinced that she would have to live with this the rest of her life. She happened to be given to an extraordinary physical therapist who recognized that the forward tilt of her head prevented her from turning. When she corrected her posture and participated in a variety of exercises she returned to normal. Notice, no drugs were used. She left a very happy person turning her neck when she wanted.

Another story on how if only all doctors did this: Two ladies checked in for physical therapy (at separate times) and they were both very sad. In fact, they were crying so my wife, a physical therapist, told them that crying was the best thing they could do and they could cry during the whole visit if they wanted. She listened to the reason they were crying and told them that she was there for them and encouraged them with positive comments. Both left with a smile on their face and a big hug for my wife.

Occupational Therapist's work with people, particularly the handicapped and the aged, to accomplish certain tasks that their infirmity makes it difficult to do. For example, with arthritic hands it may be very difficult to open a bottle cap or a jar. An OT will teach them how to use tools to do that without pain. Almost everyone as they age develop limitations and learning to live well with limitations is essential for a good life.

N. Processed Foods are Killing America

America has a major health problem with diabetes and obesity, diet caused ailments of many if not most of Americans. Many see processed foods as the major cause. Processed foods are foods that have been changed from their natural state. These can include:

- Food that is simply cut, washed, heated, pasteurized, canned, cooked, frozen, dried, dehydrated, mixed or packaged

- Food that has added preservatives and taste such as nutrients, flavor, salts, sugar or fats. Sugar is often added to enhance sales. Cheese falls into that category too. Sugar and cheese are among the worst foods for people because of their high calories, cholesterol content, and fats. Chemicals are often added to help flavors and color. These chemicals typically have no nutrition and even have some harmful impact on the human body.

Processed foods are typically in the form of frozen dinners, breakfast cereals, packaged sweets, some meats, chips and canned foods. America's desire for convenience often turns the buyer onto foods that require a minimum of preparation, unfortunately to the detriment of their health.

The European Union has some of the highest food safety standards in the world, to protect the consumer from risk that consumers could not possibly determine by themselves. Processed foods are an area of major concern. Europe has regulations to requiring manufacturers to build a healthier food base. This is also very true for medication. There are many often used prescriptions in America that are banned in Europe. American legislatures seem to ignore these major health issues even as they ignored the introduction of opioids that cause over 80,000 deaths per year. This is one of the factors for America's longevity being one of the worst in the affluent world. While opioids are terrible diabetes and obesity are far worse. Some say 25% of Americans have diabetes and 100 million are obese.

The Trump administration is the first to begin to set rules that eliminate the use of chemicals in processed foods. There is hope.

O.
Transportation Requires More Efficiency

The challenge today is to introduce less pollutants into the air. Certainly, subsidies are foolish because the government is adding to taxpayers an already out of control debt to make consumers live out what the government deems is necessary for the environment, education, or food production to name three items. But as so often happens the government is motivated by politics, false premises and false hypothesis. For example, ethanol was supposed to be the solution to lower fuel cost and clean up the environment without drilling for oil by producing fuel from corn. Time proved that a great deal of corn was necessary, causing a shortage of the most common food source that we have, which raises the cost of food. The subsidies and impact on food cost made ethanol considerably more expensive than ordinary gasoline.

EV (electric vehicles) subsidies likewise offer a false sense of savings because of the high cost of chargers, batteries, tires and the original high price of the EV. In many instances, government fails to let the consumer choose based upon the current technology and cost. Consumers will use new technology when it is attractive and economical. America doesn't need to increase our out-of-control debt to make this happen.

- Again, private enterprise has continued to increase the cost of vehicles and by using a leasing program have convinced consumers that they can enjoy the latest for just a monthly fee. So many who cannot afford a new upscale car are paying the lease without realizing they are over-paying for transportation. The car dealer makes more money leasing than he does selling a new car. This is a financial genius step by the car dealerships. They sell a lease with a down-payment. On the second lease that typically starts in 3 years, the used car's value is included in the next cars price, which can be manipulated to make major dollars. Now the car dealer has the original down-payment plus the trade-in value of the car, the value of which he sets.

- America's affluence and sprawling cities offer a challenge to improve transportation economies. Many car owners are not affluent and overspend on transportation thanks in part to the attractive leasing options that make it appear that they can afford a bigger and nicer automobile.

    Buying a new car for 3 years as compared to buying a used car for 3 years shows a major increase in cost. A rough comparison of buying a $50,000 new car vs. a $25,000 used car follows. Assuming the new car is sold for $25,000 after 3 years and the used car is sold for $10,000 after 3 years, the used car saves the buyer $25,000 in cost plus 8% in interest for 3 years which is $31,000. That does not include such cost as insurance and maintenance.

Ideal America

- In 2021, America purchased almost three times more light trucks than cars. That surprised me as it must surprise most people but pickups are a big reason. Pickups have become so popular that rumor has it that one major manufacturer has even considered dropping the manufacturing of cars. The laws governing the efficiency of cars and light trucks is requiring 2 mpg more average on a calendar schedule. Pickups have a higher fuel usage than cars but are popular because pickups have backseats and amenities. One also rides much higher in the seat making pickups more popular. Pickups are in many ways a boy toy, with power and heavy duty features similar to large trucks even though most are used for small tasks with light loads and even terrain. Many drive trucks strictly for preference, not for function.

  What can be more fun than sitting in a pickup that puts the driver almost as high as an 18-wheeler with double wide tires, lifted chassis, seating for four and even lights under the chassis? It is like a carnival ride every time. Pickups are a temptation for many men. We live in a free country so some will say that people can buy whatever they can afford and I agree with that but energy, pollution and climate must be the #1 priority in transportation so people who want pickups that use more energy should pay an extra price for that preference.

  Certainly, there is not an intent to control how people spend their money but there needs to be an incentive for driving an efficient pickup. Whether through taxation or rules, government should provide more incentive to make pickups more efficient.

- We should be pushing more efficient engines, especially hybrids that are nearly twice as efficient and the technology is sure and available. I question why the government is paying people for electric cars that are very expensive and have high maintenance cost instead of hybrids that are a proven technology and use half the gas that hydrocarbon engines use. Hybrids do not have the many problems of EV's. Hybrids don't need a charging station and the tires last longer, but the battery replacement is much higher as with EV battery replacement costing between $1000 and $6,000.

- No subsidies for electric cars. Subsidies are another waste of government money increasing the debt every day and every hour. Let the technology advance to make that form of transportation of interest to buyers because of the features, economy or concern for the environment. China is selling many electric cars but they are small and inexpensive and start at $12,000. Why not start using the EV with a small car and upgrade it for on the road travel? That would be a great place to start enabling local transportation to be inexpensive and useful to everyone. Students could drive to school. People could go shopping, all without driving a $50,000 car using a gallon every 25 miles. America would not need subsidies if inexpensive EV's were available.

- Subsidies often do not work as ethanol proved raising the price of food, created pollution and was not as good for engines as regular fuel. Now we are doing the same thing with EV's. The cost of electricity is considered almost free and it isn't. The cost of a charging station in your garage, battery and tire replacements (which are many times more expensive) does not warrant the government subsidies because they further raise the cost to taxpayers. Before you buy an electric car check the battery replacement cost. According to Elon Musk, the batteries vary with the model but he gave $5000 to $7000 as the difference. I use $1500 or less of gas each year so that represents 4 years of gas less the cost of electricity used and the charger that I need for my garage.

- Government is trying to force EV cars on the consumer but the success is very marginal because:
    » 66% of US car dealers don't have any EVs to sell, and 45% said they wouldn't sell them no matter what.
    » Affordability remains the top reason consumers aren't buying EVs.
    » EVs are very limited for long distance driving.
    » A lack of charging stations was cited as a top roadblock in 2021. People have to buy their own chargers, which are expensive and there are no distributions of charging stations around the country that makes it impractical to drive long distances with an EV.
    » Automotive companies are struggling to meet EV customer demands given ongoing supply chain issues, battery availability, chip

shortages, and increased interest in EVs exacerbated by rising gasoline prices.
  - » Many new vehicle shoppers are becoming more adamant about their decision to not consider an EV for their next purchase.
  - » The materials used on batteries (such a big part of the expense for building an EV) is not found in America so we depend upon other countries, particularly China for that material.

- For larger cars, use the hydrocarbon engine, preferably the hybrid type until such time that electric driven car technology makes if beneficial to the user.

- Problems in manufacturing the EV makes it a difficult problem for America because of the materials needed. The availability of such items as lithium is almost non-existent in America so that makes us very dependent upon other countries, especially China. Let technology prove itself before the government pays the consumer to use it. Subsidies are merely a way to waste money for something that is not proven. When it is proven the customers will buy. Instead of spending money that this country does not have to push a new unproven technology, let the technology push the consumer. When technology is attractive consumers will buy it. The government paying for new technology should not be the reason you are using it.

- Public transportation is not always available but light rail and buses are a great way to save fuel and lower one's transportation cost. Public transportation is the main means of getting to work in some cities like New York and Washington, DC. That is becoming more popular but some cities like Minneapolis have not implemented the public transportation so that it pays its way. Minneapolis used the naïve idea that they did not need ticket collection when one stepped on the light rail. Result was that only 30% paid when they boarded and crime became common. The lack of supervision and system for mandatory payment puts almost all the cost on taxpayers. Only in a socialistic state would that happen. Minneapolis and St. Paul have been leaders in crime recently and their light rail crime is a leader as well. They have to put security on their light rail. That is like adding another employee on every trip, which they don't do but the spot additions of security is a major added cost.

While writing about slowing down the EV trend, I want to relate what I saw in Germany recently. They are much more equipped for electric vehicles. At many motels a charging station is available as they are at many parking locations. They are equipped to handle the new technology. Also, Germany is a much smaller places with more compact cities so driving distances is not nearly as common. Average miles driven in one year in Germany was 8452. In America 14,263 (69% more).

P.
Laws Enforced

Does any country have more laws than America. We have so many laws that are obsolete, dating back to the horse and buggy days, to say nothing about incidental laws that continue to fly out of the legislature and every government body. Just in the last Congress, 337 laws were passed. Imagine this every year for decades. The laws number far too many to be efficiently enforced. Often those enforced depend upon the biases or objectives of the enforcement agency, which can vary depending upon the Party in charge or the adequacy of the agency that offers protection. Imagine how much additional manpower it would take to enforce 337 laws throughout the United States. At least when a law is passed two should be deleted. There are so many forgotten and unenforced laws that no one would notice.

Many laws are not enforced simply because our justice system does not have the staff to handle the many complaints.

An instance comes to mind where an investment advisor recommended a purchase guaranteeing results but when the results didn't occur, he walked away from that guarantee. Bringing the police into that situation required state involvement and their activity was so high that after one year nothing had been done and they had really put it on the shelf with no plan to pursue the crime. One's only choice then was to hire an attorney, an expensive and risky option. One often has to just accept the loss.

This sounds like a victimless crime, or at least only one but the person who did this had done it many times and totaled millions in doing it. How many robberies amount to millions of dollars stolen? Police respond to robberies why not fraud?

Another example was embezzlement. I was a victim of a very large crime of embezzlement. As a result, I eventually spoke over 40 times to groups about embezzlement. I learned that embezzlement was a very common crime occurring not just in the obvious place of businesses but in such places as golf course management, churches, gun clubs, and even the IRS. The numbers were staggering. No doubt anywhere people handle money that was not their own, the temptation to take some of the money is always there and some devoid of principles choose to help themselves.

I will never forget sharing the podium with a female from the Minneapolis police force. Her first words were, "If you experience the crime of embezzlement, don't call us." Then she explained how hard it was to indict embezzlers. A number of people who shared their experience to me said they spent more in loss time providing documentation, employee time for evidence, testifying, etc. than the amount embezzled. That is a double loss. Also, it was ironic to me that most embezzlers are later employed in a financial assignment that provides all the elements for future embezzlement.

And then we have laws, such as illegal immigration, that were ignored to the mind-boggling amounts of millions every year. Has any crime been more numerous or more purposely ignored? In the recent administration, there seemed to be purpose to increase illegal immigration. No one could possibly change the rules to allow doubling and tripling of a crime such as illegal immigration without purpose and intent.

We also have a relatively new breed of prosecutors and judges who chose which laws they will enforce and which they will ignore. The multi-billionaire Hungarian George Soros, now a United States citizen, has an international purpose to change or even cancel democracy. Many say he has funded large amounts to such law enforcement positions as attorney generals who have chosen to select what crimes they will pursue and in some cases they are even violent crimes. These new liberal attorney generals have even reduced or eliminated the bond process that insures the indicted person attendance to future court proceedings. Even violent crimes are treated with soft bails and enforcement processes.

While he was very soft on common crimes, the NYC attorney general, funded by George Soros for election, and the federal attorney Jack Smith, used millions of dollars to pursue a victimless crime against Donald Trump that was questionable. Smith pursued the charges that in a Party atmosphere, which was so biased, many viewed as a political attack. The time and effort that was spent on the alleged charges would have covered hundreds of common crimes normally prosecuted. In the end, the violations of the trial were so great that most attorneys believed an appeal of the decision would have been easily overturned. Instead, the prosecuted was elected president so the likelihood of the trial being useful would hardly ever be realized, but the reputation of those conducting the witch hunt will never be revived.

In the case of NYC, this George Soros funded attorney general who spent enormous amounts of time and taxpayer money to pursue a political based trial, chose to ignore many crimes such as theft and even violent crimes.

How does our country arrive at a fair and consistent judicial system? There is no sense in crimes in one state or city being ignored while being prosecuted in another. There is no sense in having laws protecting citizens ignored wasting the public's trust while laws that are politically motivated are pursued vigorously at an expense much greater than violent crime.

For our country to be consistent, the federal government needs to take charge but that poses many additional problems as we know from watching government handle such things as government, drugs, immigration and many other crimes. Only the legislature (rather than the Federal Department of Justice) can impact this problem. For example, laws must be passed requiring our government to enforce such laws as immigration. If the justice system chooses to ignore laws that are so critical to this nation, impeachment should be automatic rather than a political process.

Perhaps there should be laws requiring counties, cities and states to have a common justice system for the laws rather than depending upon the political climate and biases of each county, city or state.

Q.
Crime Greatly Reduced

The citizens in America have been under the impression that they can be safe in America but that notion has passed, especially in our cities. The murder rates, looting, carjacking, rapes, and all other crimes have blossomed in the last few decades, especially the last decade. Murders in the major cities have gotten worse since Black Lives Matter has come aboard, and ironically among the black population. Those murders have been predominantly blacks being murdered by blacks. The BLM mentality has raised the murder rate of blacks, which is the total opposite of what the name implies.

It seems incredulous but many of our cities have actually tried to reduce the police force and disrespect their work. That has only resulted in more crime as many policemen have retired early or found a job where the city respected their work and punished the criminal. As the George Soros funded attorney generals have won, the justice system has stepped back and sought to be 'forgiving' of the criminal and reduce or eliminate the punishment.

Those policemen who stay in their job have taken a less caring attitude realizing that their work was often ineffective due to the justice system turning into a criminal slanted process. Secondly, because of the defunding and so many policemen leaving, they do not have the manpower to respond to many crimes. If the justice system releases many of those arrested, why waste time and perhaps even expose one's life to a dangerous situation for nought?

Safety of our citizens has diminished especially since 2020. Some have tried to cut back on the police force resulting in a substantial increase in crime that was already embarrassingly high. The cutback was a false savings. Instead of paying policemen from taxes, victims pay directly to the criminal when robbed with their property and/or their life.

What are the crimes we face in America?

- Murder rates – In 2023, America had 21,156 people die of homicide, a rate of 6.3 homicides per 100,000 population. On a comparison with other affluent nations, the United States has the highest homicide rate. Outside of Mexico, United States was the only country with cities ranking among the top seven most dangerous cities in the world. Minneapolis recently was the #1 crime city in America with St. Paul being #2 so Chicago is not by itself.

- To my surprise, deaths due to drugs was much more disastrous than homicides. In 2022, 107,941 people died from a drug overdose; 82,000 due to opioids. Strangely the FDA approved the drug that now out numbers all other drugs in deaths. Does that say something about our federal government and their bureaucracies? Many of the executives in the FDA change jobs and work for the pharmaceutical companies. The department that governs drugs has a very friendly relationship with the manufacturers whose product is being policed by the FDA.

- Looting has increased 19% in the last 5 years due in part, to the results of government reaction to the

George Floyd event. As previously stated in this book, some city governments have blamed the police for unrest showed by the protests. They have reacted by defunding and disrespecting the police. Since looting was normally not a dangerous crime, this crime has been last to be enforced with an understaffed police force. There has even been mass looting where 25 or more people put on masks and go into a store together and openly grab large amounts of products from the store. No store can protect themselves with that type of surprise attack. As a result of this looting problem, many stores have closed in areas where looting persists. The cost of looting in America is in the billions of dollars. Of course, that impacts the cost of goods for all of America. Consumers really pay for the looting crime.

- Carjacking is a dangerous crime because the criminal uses a weapon to openly steal the car. In one year, Minneapolis had 600 car jackings. People were almost scared to go into a parking ramp to get their car fearing that they would be attacked. In 2022, 27 homicides occurred during carjackings, which clearly emphasizes the danger.
- Scams seem to be everywhere. My emails contain a scam attempt almost every day. A false purchase or invoice attempt occurs frequently. A list of scams is:
    » advance fee schemes,
    » Ponzi schemes,
    » pyramid schemes,
    » telemarketing fraud scams,
    » phishing schemes,

- » voice phishing schemes,
- » identity theft,
- » investment scams,
- » cryptocurrency scams,
- » impersonation scams,
- » blackmail,
- » romance,
- » selling non-existent items,
- » E-commerce and
- » delivery scams.

Warning signs include:

- Claiming to be from the government, a bank, a business, or a family member asking for money
- Asking for money up front to receive a prize or a gift
- Asking for money by wire, courier, or credit card. In one experience of mine, the address was an empty parking lot
- Asking for a credit card number, ATM security code, or any security access to money or property
- Taking ownership of property through manipulation
- Even what appears to be legitimate purchase from a local seller can be a form of scam when they use a card according to their rules
- Of particular concern are the scams used on our senior citizens many of whom do not have the skills to detect a scam.
- Because of these many crimes, the citizens of the United States no longer feel safe especially in the cities where shootings in the night are almost common.

John Benedict

What can Americans do?

- Vote for justice systems and legislatures that believe in protecting citizens
- Chase the George Soros type billionaires out of America
- Treat all people the same instead of designing a law enforcement system on how to be elected
- Reject crime
- Support religions that believe in honesty, respect, and protection of the people in this country.

R.
Caring for the Poor, Sick, Mentally Handicapped and Those Suffering Crises.

America needs to take care of those who cannot provide for themselves. We have struggled in that area for years and I believe it is getting worse.

Homeless – in United States we have some cities with 770,000 homeless people. There are whole communities of homeless and they are often mentally ill, addicted to drugs, sick, hungry and lost. They often are victims of criminals as well. That is a very sad situation that should not happen in America.

Homelessness has risen a record in 2024, 18% greater than last year and 36% greater than 2019. The blue states have vastly out done the red states in growth. For example, New York has increased 70% and Illinois has increased 153% in homelessness.

By contrast, Texas, a red state has a very small increase in homelessness of 8% even though they are the most subject to illegal immigration.

One factor is the illegal migration. Blue states are sanctuary cities attracting the illegal migrants. Also the laws in the Blue states are more liberal attracting the homeless.

What are solutions?

- Treatment and regulations for the mentally ill and those who are addicted of drugs and alcohol. These are addressed later in this chapter. This country has provided very poor support for the mentally handicapped and those who addicted.

- Cut the distribution of drugs. This country is a bonanza for the drug trade. There are countries with laws so strong that the use of drugs is almost nonexistent.

- Control immigration rather than having immigration control America. Allowing 10 to 20 million illegal immigrants into America in the Biden term is perhaps a record for breaking America's laws and breaking the immigration laws leads to untold number of other crimes, rape, murder, torture, sex trafficking, crime gangs in our cities, looting car-jacking, and the list goes on.

- There are over 7000 federal buildings going to waste and other buildings neither in use or salable. Inexpensive buildings can be constructed that serve as dormitories.

- Make the homeless available for adoption, so to speak, allowing people to volunteer to care for a homeless person not necessarily in their home but where they stay. People have a way of taking care of one person, not necessarily housing but for food, shelter, and medical needs. I have learned that some people are just incapable of taking care of themselves and need help.

Mentally ill – at one time we had mental institutions until some believed that they should not be locked into a facility so they were let loose and the mental institutions disappeared except for the criminally insane who are dangerous and locked behind bars. Many of those mentally ill became homeless living in very poor and even dangerous conditions.

We have facilities for the criminally insane. We need facilities for those who have mental issues so great that they cannot care for themselves. We need to rebuild facilities and employ personnel to do that on a higher level than those of decades ago. Instead of eliminating mental institutions we should have revised them to solve the respect and freedom issues that motivated the elimination of mental institutions.

Hungry – many churches and other organizations feed the homeless and the homeless know where and when those meals are available. I am unaware whether hunger is the major issue with the homeless.

Sick – a lack of health care for homeless and even the poor living in a home occurs too often. When Americans are sick and suffering from a disease such as diabetes or heart problems, we must find a way to take care of them better than we are.

I have no idea how providing human care to these unfortunate Americans can be satisfied but America needs to be responsible and find solutions whether by legislation at the federal level or by a state agreement that is uniform throughout America. States and cities need to be organized and governed to help these people.

In regard to people suffering because of hurricanes, forest fires, earthquakes, floods, tornadoes and all the unexpected disasters what part should the government play. We are having more mishandled crises now.

But the need to respond to floods and hurricanes on a timely basis has become inadequate and the bureaucracy of the federal government's FEMA has left many citizens without homes, power, and even food for too much time in some cases. I recognize that FEMA has a major challenge in facing unscheduled problems such as hurricanes. They need competent, trained, and organized part-time workers, yes, a difficult assignment but they also need a money supply sufficient for the crisis.

However, it was disheartening to see another federal agency go political as they did in a recent crisis. Management told some workers to bypass homes with Trump signs. We have politics in our justice system, tax system and now FEMA??? Government is assigned the task of helping America not some political Party.

Government is not good in meeting those challenges. I don't know what the solutions are for FEMA but it should involve a sufficient number of private businesses and individuals who are available at a moment's notice to respond to disasters. This would be similar to the National Guard who responds almost instantly when they are needed.

5.
Racism Needs a Soft Landing

We hear the word 'racist' far too often. 'Racist' is a political strategy to capture the black vote. By using that word so often, the country keeps the thought of racism alive and keeps those who believe it, convinced that only one Party is responsible for freedom in that community. The word racism has been pounded into the head of most blacks that live in a black community. Not so much to those living in other communities who are immune to the racist idea.

There is an idiom that says if you hear a lie often enough you will believe it and racism falls into that truth. I believe that if the word was never said again, there would be a major impact on the feelings that are generated.

The absurdity of using the word is illustrated by the political battles in the large cities that are almost totally governed by Democrats who have captured the market to such a degree that the Republicans are non-competitive and seldom even have someone on the city council. Yet in competing, the Democrats use racist to describe the Republicans even though Republicans are not a threat. That seems to convince the uneducated that Democrats are on their side and even though in their community the crime is very high and the education very bad, they vote Democrat.

John Benedict

I had an interesting encounter with the racist word. In a choral group, I developed a friendship with a lawyer who was a Democrat. I had always wanted to exchange political views with a Democrat so I suggested we meet for breakfast every Saturday and talk politics. Of course, we didn't just talk politics but other things as friends would do. As early as the 2nd or 3rd meeting, we discussed a political issue on which we disagreed and we did that without rancor or partisan attitude. To my great surprise, he out of the blue, called me a racist. We weren't even talking about race and my history being raised in Nebraska that had one black family in the whole county, worked in Detroit with black workers and was even married by a black minister proves this accusation was purely a defensive fallback position.

We continued to meet since I did not take offense at his remark. However eventually, the word was used again vehemently and I ended the meetings and the relationship. I found that when he had no argument on a political issue his fallback position was to call me a racist. That is not uncommon.

The frequent use of the word racist keeps the word and the thought alive. I live in a very mixed neighborhood of blacks, Hispanics and Caucasian where the word and the action are not used. We don't really think of race as we are neighbors and frequently speak and perform neighborly assistance.

The country has a history of trying to treat other races and ethnic groups in a preferential position that in a way penalizes some races, even keeps the word racist alive. It seems all ethnic differences are publicly exploited in the beginning but disappear after a few decades. Good examples are the Irish and the Italians.

There is an effort to keep the same ratio in everything from education to jobs. For example, in sports, there was much discussion and even rules by the NFL for coaches being in the same ratio as the nation's race. That is somewhat humorous when you see that the players were very much out of balance especially in basketball where the black players are nearly 80% of all players.

In education, efforts have been made to allow lower grades for some races to achieve graduation, which corrupts all of education and also lessens the performance of the black community treating them as lesser people. Lowering the standards does no one a favor. That only makes the numbers look better. You might say it is a political move. Instead, perhaps the educational community needs to improve their performance.

Is prejudice alive today? Certainly, but it isn't limited to the black or Hispanic communities. Many are prejudiced against Jews, obese, poor and even rich people. Prejudice is a human failure. Human nature does that. In black communities there is prejudice against Caucasians. The Natural man looks at the outside instead of the heart and makes judgments that are not of God. Racism is not only a political statement but signs of a twisted heart.

One of the most racist bills ever that had a huge negative affect on race is LBJ's War on Poverty bill passed during the mid-60's. That bill used welfare to fund black women (as well as others) so that they could have and raise children without a father. That allowed men to become door to door Romeo's and not take responsibility for impregnating a woman. That has resulted in 80% of blacks in some communities not even knowing who was their father. As one might expect, without a father young men do not attain an element of discipline and responsibility resulting in a lack of work ethics and a tendency toward crime. That may be the main reason our cities experience so much rampant crime. Unfortunately, fatherless children perpetuate many problems that exists in our black communities.

How does our country address this problem that is more a tool than a fact? Of course, those who are believers in God must, as part of their faith, treat all people the same from the act of love instead of judgment. Since a large percent of America claim to belong to a religion, that alone would accomplish the act of eliminating racist actions. However, faith does not always eliminate all sin because believers still sin.

So, for those people of faith who are still biased and for those many who are truly biased, we just need to use discipline to not even use the word. The Democratic Party in particular must stop using race as a political strategy and the media must stop using the word in an effort to draw attention to the negative.

There also is a movement supported by the Supreme Court to eliminate diversity requirements, which will help eliminate the racist idea as well.

T.
Religion Encouraged

We have the separation of church and state amendment and that is an important one but we should not treat religion as a concept that is un-American. We should be open to it and not make attempts to curtail publications, signs and employ extreme rules about using prayer and signs of religion in public places. We certainly should not close down churches for reasons improperly researched such as the government did with COVID. The COVID rules had an impact on church attendance that still exists a few years after COVID is no longer a problem.

At the same time, we need to not place those who profess no faith or another faith in a position where they have to participate in a belief system with which they do not support. An example of making faith mandatory in government rules is exemplified by many Muslim countries and it does so to their detriment.

What does religion do for this country?

- Religion promotes civil behavior that is very helpful to the community and reduces crimes and unacceptable behavior. The Ten Commandments for example are rules that are very healthy for our country. The entire Bible teaches good behavior and neighborly relationships. Christian doctrine expands upon those ways of life. Note that crime is very low in strong Christian communities.

- The amount of money and personal assistance in this country by religious organizations is very helpful to those in need. Many churches help the homeless, feed the hungry, care for the helpless, provide medical support and educate those without. How much is given is impossible to know since many Christians give personally or directly. The number is estimated to be in the billions. Every church in some way provides these services. Some of the bigger churches provide a huge amount of support to those in need.

- Religion needs to be considered a positive in America even to atheists. They need to see the benefits and not make rules to handicap those who have a faith in God. Ironically, atheists are religious too. The definition of religion is a belief system and atheists have belief systems too, that there is no God.

U.
Free Speech for All Not Just Protesters

Free speech is a very important freedom in America. It is rooted to prevent the silencing of people concerned about the direction of the nation. Free speech is given to news programs who report biased news depending often on their political beliefs. That is, the media enjoys free speech since they often deceive the viewers with unbalanced and inaccurate reporting. That deception is acceptable because we consider it free speech. This rule makes sense since the news is a voluntary choice.

Free speech cannot be an excuse to disrupt American progress. Campus and street protests interfere with other Americans who are engaged in American business. For example, if you are on a campus for education or on streets and roads traveling to your destination, protests will disrupt your day including interrupting your free speech. Your transportation, work, silence time and views are attacked. That is not voluntary. We do not choose it. Those who protests are violating our freedoms, work and education. That should not be allowed.

Protesters shout free speech as they take over campuses, streets and even freeways at times but their actions take away the free speech of many who love America and speak out of respect. Most evident are college campuses where it seems presidents of universities and professors are on the side of the protesters regardless of the damage that they do or the positions that they hold. There have been many conservative speakers kept off of campus events because the administration is biased and/or the liberal element creates chaos when conservatives are on campus for a speech or event.

Then we also have the LGBTQ citizens wanting to dictate speech by others outside of their community. When I first heard that the LGBTQ community wanted all Americans to use the pronouns, they choose for themselves I was in shock. For example, a man that claims to be a girl wants to be called a she and to disregard language that we have used since the beginning of time to honor their foreign lifestyle. That is hardly free speech.

The most extreme example are the Gaza protests. Imagine protesting for Hamas, a terrorist organization that went across the border into Israel, killed, tortured and kidnapped innocents. Allowing that element to disrupt and replace free speech is beyond my understanding. The Gaza protests were initially allowed to be on campus, even set up residence on campus sites interrupting those attending classes and attempting to receive an education. There is no reason that such protests should be allowed on campus.

What is ironic and also reveals the intelligence of some Gaza protesters is that some protesters are LGBTQ and don't know that in Gaza they could be executed for being LGBTQ. Does one get the idea that some people protest just out of rebellion, desire to destroy property without being arrested, gain attention, and be on the local news. And to think this is all allowed to honor "free speech."

Free speech is a right but interrupting free speech by Americans is an offense to our Constitution and America.

V.
Immigration

Immigration laws in America have been changing over the years since 1790. I have listed a few that are germane to our existing immigration problems.

- The first is from the 14th amendment ratified on 1868. This was closely connected with freedom of the slaves and made them citizens. The Amendment has one item that grants citizenship to all persons born or naturalized in the United States, including formerly enslaved people.

- The Chy Lung v. Freeman act of 1880 affirmed that the federal government holds sole authority to regulate immigration. Are you listening sanctuary cities?

- The immigration act of 1882 ruled that convicts, lunatics and those likely to become a public charge were not eligible to immigration into the USA.

- US Supreme Court ruled in 1898 that any person born in the United States is a citizen by birth regardless of race or parent's status.

- Blease's Law of 1929 criminalized crossing the border outside an official port of entry.

- Passed in October 2006, this law mandated that the Secretary of Homeland Security act quickly to achieve operational control over U.S. international land and maritime borders including an expansion of existing walls, fences, and surveillance.
- Homeland Security Act was passed in 2002, creating the Department of Homeland Security (DHS) by consolidating 22 diverse agencies and bureaus. The creation of DHS reflected mounting anxieties about immigration in the aftermath of the terrorist attacks of September 11th.

Immigration law has been controversial and very partisan for decades and because of the great difference between the two parties, very little law has been made in recent decades. The differences seem to be more political than purposeful for America. Many believe that flooding America with illegal immigrants will somewhere in the future provide more votes for one party.

Immigration has been an issue that has not gathered unified thoughts from Americans until 2020 when Trump began to build the wall to control illegal immigrants better. The 2020 election put a Party in the White house that had the opposite intention that essentially opened up the border.

Under Trump, the illegal immigrants were far too many but he was able to diminish the number considerably and begin to get the border under control. However, the following administration took away much of that control and nearly opened up the border to anyone ignoring the laws of America. The number of illegals arrested in 2021 was 3 times greater than 2020 and 4 times greater in 2022 than 2020.

Ideal America

This created major problems for America;

- America had no system for processing and absorbing such level of immigrants.
- The judicial system and the border guards are inadequate for such a flood of illegal immigrants so they cannot do a proper job to prosecute those who are violating the law. Our laws cannot be enforced. Too many people.
- Housing became a major problem since the existing housing was totally inadequate so the government turned them loose with responsibility to stay in touch. Of course, hardly any of them do. They are lost in America and our DHS does not know where they are.
- Feeding those coming across the border set up a welfare arm
- The young immigrants require education according to USA law so that is another major cost and responsibility complicated by the language differences.
- The added cost to the federal government, state, and cities became overwhelming.
- Homeless multiplied
- Many American jobs were taken by the illegal immigrants at a much lower cost
- Crime increased immeasurably because sanctuary cities did not notify nor would they release the arrests of illegal immigrants. So there were many

cases of illegals being arrested, released and then committing a more violent crime. Some countries like Venezuela released criminals and pointed them to the United States.

- About 400 known terrorists were admitted into this country raising concerns about terrorists' attacks.
- The added costs of illegal immigrants in the United States is approaching ½ trillion dollars for the last 4 years.
- Farmers with land on the border suffer from frequent criminal actions by illegal immigrants.
- The mass of illegal immigrants has made the cartels a 20-billion-dollar business. They demand payment from them, rob them rape and murder some. Many young people are forced into sex trafficking, forced labor and treated as slaves.
- The flood of immigrants also makes the smuggling of drugs easier.
- The administration of 2021 to Jan. 2025 is spending money much of it secretly to fly illegal immigrants to places all over America at night. In many cases they are buying hotel rooms for them to stay, feeding and even educating some. All of this to support the crime of illegal immigration.

What about all the people in this world who are looking for a better life? Some are opportunist but many are living in a repressive government, some are just trying to find a better life.

Ideal America

First of all, America has several times passed a bill to import people from a country that is in serious trouble. But that can only be an exception not the open borders that we have had between 2021 and 2025 of January.

My answer to the question wanting charity to everyone that wants a better life is how many in the world fall in that category? The answer would be in the billions. Using that philosophy, Los Angeles would be easily 100 million people. Fort Myers/Cape Coral would be 20 million. Then what would happen to the life style in America and to the opportunities? We would no longer be America with opportunity, freedom to succeed and financially we would be in even worse shape than we are now.

If that is the wish of the majority of Americans, then there would be a legal way to do it. if you feel that way, find candidates to run our government that would endorse that idea and help them win, but only using American laws and freedoms.

Why would anyone support illegal immigration? That is a crime. America has ways for people who want to become citizens. To those who say it is too hard, then change it but keep it where America is in control, where criminals, terrorists, people with no job skills, and people looking for a welfare check cannot just walk into this country and become dependent on our food, education, medical treatment, and life.

What an be done to bring this flood of immigrants under control and in obedience to American Law?

- Stop the illegal invasion with a wall, additional border guards and as many people as necessary to protect Americans, the farmers that live on the border and as a bonus stop the drug smuggling.

- Eliminate sanctuary cities and states that seem to believe they have federal power.
- Find and deport first, all terrorists and criminals. That includes those that are in sanctuary cities who are not immune from Federal Law.
- Find the criminal insane and other illegal immigrants that are a danger to America and deport them
- Find the children who are being used for sex trafficking and forced labor. Give them freedom and a protected environment. Find all of the lost children and make sure they are given care and direction.
- Find all the gangs with illegal immigrants, dismantle, jail and deport as required.
- Add additional staff to the justice system in charge of illegal immigrants and catch up on the legal process for immigrants.
- Find all illegals who have disappeared from our governance. Organize a path for them whether to deport them or adapt them into a productive and legal immigration process.
- Require all illegals to meet their commitments on location and reporting to the justice system.
- Create more up to date laws on a bipartisan basis. These laws should represent what Americans want for immigrants – their credentials,

Immigration has become one of the top issues in America and has to be put under control.

W.
States Govern to Keep Citizens Safe and Prosperous

States have their own government. They have their own laws, infrastructure responsibilities, tax collection, property management, state patrol, universities, and like the federal government they fund counties and cities to some degree.

Responsibilities of states are best understood by looking at their budget.

Income in the form of taxes are:
- Liquor/tobacco
- Property
- Corporate
- Sales
- Income

Expenses are:
- Public safety including state patrol
- Transportation – highways, light rail etc.
- Attorney General justice system
- Judiciary system including State Supreme court
- Environment rules and supervision
- Elections
- Agriculture and Housing

- » Jobs
- » Education for elementary and high school
- » Universities
- » Some veteram and government employee support

States vary a great deal in their system. Minnesota, New York, Illinois and California are quite socialistic taking responsibility that would otherwise be taken by individuals. Free meals at school, health assistance, transportation, and many other items that in a democratic system is handled by the individual.

With socialistic systems the cost balloons compared to a democratic system. For example, the cost per person for government in Florida is 40% the cost of that in Minnesota. Nothing is free and when government taxes citizens for the money, creates a department to handle, provides support of their gifts the cost is much greater. Like mowing your lawn. It is cheap when you do it yourself and very expensive when you hire it done. Of course, Government does not operate on a profit basis so their efficiency is much less than with a private system.

EDUCATION

The highest cost for many states is education. Not only do they fund the universities entirely but they subsidize K-12. No entity has more influence over government in many states than education. For example, in Minnesota, education is almost 40% of the state's total cost and Health is almost 30%, leaving only 30% for the entire rest of the State responsibility.

As I wrote earlier, the legislature passed a bill to feed every K-12 student TWO meals every day. They passed several high-priced socialistic items such as free meals for students, breakfast and lunch.

Minnesota's 2024 budget was a disaster. As Jim Abeler, a Senator in Minnesota wrote, "The reality is that the Trifecta leaders worked alone, ignoring all advice from across the aisle, to increase spending to astronomical levels. They paid no heed to those with sage fiscal savvy and worked in secret while going on the spending spree of a lifetime.

In their haste to buy virtually every trinket in the store, they neglected to adequately fund the very things Minnesotans rely on: hospitals, nursing homes, and even medical transportation for needy persons getting blood transfusions and dialysis.

And in awarding record-breaking funding for schools, they didn't listen to the experts in the school districts on how to usefully allocate that spending. Tragically, in the face of receiving two to three times the usual funding increase, nearly every district is cutting teachers and staff while fewer than half of the students can read and do math at grade level."

After raising the 2024 budget over 25%, enjoying 17 billion of an $18 billion surplus the year before which they captured for 2024, and increasing taxes they even now have a $5 billion deficit for the year just ahead.

They passed several high-priced socialistic items such as free meals for students, breakfast and lunch.

The education lobby is second to none. They almost control state government. Each year their contribution to education goes up and yet the results are going down. Back to my chapter on education becoming private. States would save enormous amounts of money.

CRIME CONTROL

States seem to have no impact on crime control. Cities struggle a great deal but I do not see States helping the situation.

Is it right to have states differ so much on their taxes and services? I believe it is wrong but the arguments between the left and the right are very strong. Where would you standardize and how? No idea.

I see so much crime in our cities and the State does not seem to be involved. Shouldn't the National Guard or some external force be used to round up the gangs that seem to be uncontrolled by the City Police?

X.
Corporations - Get Over the Greed

Much of our life is determined by the corporations that provide so many products and services to us. We are dependent on their quality and integrity. However, there has been a trend toward corporate greed and manipulation that takes advantage of the buyer. They do this by monopolistic trends and contracts that is unyielding to consumers who cannot afford to hire an attorney to evaluate the authenticity and fairness of contracts.

ONE SIDED CONTRACTS

Typically, corporations want your credit card number and want you to agree with their terms and conditions before proceeding. The credit card number gives them carte blanche regardless of performance and the conditions protect them from any legal challenges. Large companies have large staffs to defend their contracts and endless amount of money to pursue any legal issues. The simple customer has no such funds and no realistic defense when they realize the corporation has taken advantage of them.

Examples:

- My first book was contracted with Westbow Press publishing. I chose them because they were recommended by a friend and I did the common but stupid thing: I trusted them. I contracted with them for about $15,000 to publish the book and do some marketing. They told me they would take 3 months. The contract required that I pay 1/3 for each of the first three months so they had all their money in the first three months. This is very common payment terms in the publishing industry. Actually, they have your money in 2 months since at the inception of the contract they used the credit card for the first payment. The third payment was made two months down the road so they were completely paid via my credit card in just 2 months.

It took them 6 months just to edit the book. They estimated 2 weeks. The cover design was estimated to take only a few weeks after that. After the editing they stated that the cover design would not start for another month or two and based on how they performed the editing that estimate could not be trusted. I have since had a book cover made in one week.

In addition, as the editing was completed, I received a call from Westbow proposing a more sophisticated marketing plan for over $13,000. Again, the charge would be made to my credit card in the first 2 months and no results were guaranteed. That attempt to glean more money with no guarantee of results from a company who had already proven they were unreliable was the straw that broke the camel's back. I had lost all faith in Westbow and realized they were ignoring their own performance. They were just trying to sell another product with no guarantee of performance with money that was not refundable if they did not perform.

By this time, I realized that continuing with Westbow was an extremely big risk. Contracting with a publisher I reasoned was somewhat like a marriage. I would be very dependent upon Westbow. If they did not perform before, how could I trust them to perform now? I would have just wasted more money after already wasting $15,000, so I cancelled the contract and as you might expect, they would not refund any of the money even though they had not incurred significant expense. I realized then that I could not trust them. The editing was a separate contract so Westbow essentially made off with all of my money with only the cost of a few telephone calls.

The incredible aspect of Westbow's approach is that they spent almost nothing on the tasks of publishing my book and were heading toward a completion of 10 -12 months when they estimated 3 months during the pre-contract discussion. They constructed a contract typical of so many companies, a contract that is only advantageous to Westbow. The consumer does not have the resources to hire legal assistance to either evaluate the contract before it is signed or pursue legal process to recover the money when their performance is so far from what they estimated.

Dorrance Publishing was the one that I found to do the work. They were half the price and produced close to the 3-month estimate.

- Another example: I hired a lawn service company (PestBear) stopped by and sold me on treating my grass primarily for fertilizations and weeds. The only price given was the $70 that was quoted for each month. I stipulated that the tech that performs the service must contact me when he performed the task. I had questions of course and wanted a better understanding of what specifically was being done and what I could expect.

When the tech arrived, I was in the house and he began spraying. I was expecting him to knock and contact me as requested. In only 10 minutes after he arrived, he was gone. I called and complained. An executive stopped and covered the bases with me. He verified the pricing even though his representative did not mention it. He also assured me that the next service call would make sure the tech contacted me. This was too much so I cancelled the contract. Since they had my credit card it was difficult to be treated fairly as usual.

In the meantime, I was invoiced for the second month and was unable to have that refunded. Again, the second visit was a 10-minute visit.

I was invoiced $70 for the first treatment and another surprise invoice for $63. They explained that one price was for fertilization and the other for weed treatment. They would bill these each month. This was not mentioned during my verbal contract. Once I understood they would bill $133 per month, I realized how overpriced this was. One only fertilizes the lawn a few times during the year and not during the hottest months, so $133 per month for a 10-minute visit was obscene.

I have many more illustrations of these two problems.

LEGAL ADVANTAGE

Another item to apply a great deal of caution is the one-way contracts crafted with a great deal of legal work. Large companies can afford to draft a very one-way contract for the consumer who has neither the money nor the time to review and change one-way contracts. The consumer really has no choice anyway except to accept that contract. Later if there is a disagreement the consumer has to spend thousands to hire a lawyer and fight the issue. Most purchases don't warrant that.

Along with a one-way contract the seller often requires a credit card to proceed and from that point the consumer has no buying control. About the only step that the consumer can take is to cancel the contract and that may take a great deal of time and also has to meet the legality of the crafted contract. The option of cancelling payment through the credit card company is not an easy step. In most cases they honor the contract that the vendor has leaving the consumer in a loss situation. In my experience that holds true even when no written contract exists.

Be careful to require written contracts. I was in business with municipalities and found them to be immaculate in payments. Not so with private contracts. As stated, a large corporation can, and will spend considerable money crafting a contract totally in their own favor. The consumer has little if any freedom to change that contract. Either accept it or don't buy the product and of course we are all trusting souls so we normally trust the seller to be fair when that is the least of the seller's concerns. Here are examples of both large and small sellers using the one-way contract and possession of your credit card to take advantage of the consumer:

John Benedict

- I bought an above ground pool. I had intended to install a pool in the ground and spend $80,000 but this above ground pool would suffice and the cost was only $28,000. They offered me a big discount to buy that day and the excuse was that they would then have a customer in that area as a reference. I had no intentions of buying that day but I did buy because of the discount. Only 4 days later I found a much better fit. I could buy a swimming spa for about the same price and it offered significant advantages. I went back to cancel the contract for the above ground pool and their contract would not allow cancellation after 3 days. I had placed a down payment of $1000 on the pool but I decided to give up the $1000 rather than buy the above ground pool. I then began getting telephone calls from the seller pressing me and adding the fact that on page 3 of the contract it said that cancellation charges after 3 days was 25% of the contract. I dug in my heels and said we would just have to go to court and refused to talk to them anymore. It took a while but they gave in and even refunded my $1000. That contract however communicates how one-sided a contract can be. They would not have incurred any cost on that pool for maybe weeks so the 3 days was a typical one-sided seller contract.
- Even verbal contracts can be bad. I had a rental home that suddenly needed a sewage blockage cleaned. I called Roto-Rooter who arrived the next day. I lived 1800 miles away so all of this was by phone. When the service tech was on the site, he called to tell me that the line was blocked to the street and also to the tub. The cost would be over $1200. I felt I had no choice except to tell him to go ahead. He wanted a credit card and I gave him the card numbers.

He proceeded. However, the renter told me he was gone in one hour, which means he lied to me. Essentially, he was charging over $1200 an hour. I argued with Roto-Rooter for quite some time. They insisted that when they gave me a quote and I gave them a credit card that was a contract regardless of the time that they spent on the job. Roto-Rooter obviously didn't care what was fair only what advantage they had to make double or triple what was normal. We had quite a verbal battle and they finally lowered the cost to about $800, which would have been just for the line out to the street, still a ridiculous charge.

- I have had this happen on other service work. A plumber gave me a price for a task and it was about double what he needed. This process of giving an estimate, receiving a credit card number and considering that a contract is in many ways a scam. They estimate the worst-case scenario of course, so they make often times double the fair price. Make sure you question any seller who quotes a price and wants your credit card number. Be sure they do not claim this is a contract. If they insist upon it, you would profit by finding another seller who does not require a credit card.

CUSTOMER SERVICE

One of the big irritants of my life is calling companies to answer a question or get direction. I might have a question such as the computer wants a code and I don't have one. Their automated phone system typically does not give that question as an option only common questions mostly on payment. No matter what you say, the system will not give you direction unless it is one of the few items the automation will handle. They never give an option to talk to a live person. You might spend 10 minutes just trying to get past the automated phone system so that you can talk to someone. There isn't just one menu but you may have to deal with several before you are connected with a live person.

This really is designed to save the company money so they do not have to pay any live person's time. Once they program the computer that interface with the customer is practically free. But the time that the customer spends trying to get an answer is not free to the customer. Instead of spending 5 minutes or even 1 minute in many cases, the customer might spend as much as half an hour to find a simple answer that would take 15 seconds to give. I have several times spent a full hour to get a simple answer that a knowledgeable person could have given to me in 15 seconds.

This is not the last problem. Once you are given a path to a live person, one has to wait for that person to be available. The computerized system frequently says the live person is tied up and will call you back, which sometimes they do and sometimes they don't. The person often is from overseas, particularly the Philippines. They speak broken English but some pronunciations do not sound at all as it does in America and a 15,000-mile communication line is not the clearest communication either. The communication then becomes difficult because a key word has to be repeated several times and explained. I have often had to ask for someone that I can understand. Secondly, the Filipino person often is similar to the computer in his limited responses. They are programmed to answer only certain questions and beyond that you have to insist upon a supervisor, which is another time-consuming effort.

Customer service is provided by companies at their convenience and in that way costing the consumer a great deal of time and many consumers just give up.

EMPLOYMENT FACTORS

Some corporations have human resource divisions that bully the employee especially when dismissing them from their employment. Once again, they have legal resources that the employee cannot match without spending a large percentage of their own money.

Human resource divisions take advantage of their position. For example, quite often the employee is dismissed when their supervisor is the one that should be dismissed. The employee is then mistreated but has no choice unless he hires an attorney. This happens more than one would think.

How are Human Resource departments unfair with severance issues? They use severance pay for leverage and threaten the employee to sign a dismissal contract guaranteeing that the employee will not take legal action against the company for an unfair action. They can do this by refusing to pay any severance pay for example and there are other financial actions they can use to threaten the employee as well. They can also threaten to provide a negative reference.

This mirrors the unequal contracts that corporations use while the buyer has no legal advice without spending an inordinate amount of money.

Some large corporations have mammoth legal capability to use against employees who have no knowledge how to defend themselves just as they do with buyers.

How can one evaluate how many corporations violate employment laws and fairness? Just look at the number of employment lawyers. They are all making very good money on the illegalities of big corporations. But unfortunately, the victim cannot afford a lawyer or doesn't even know they have that choice.

Another instance of bullying by a large corporation of its employees that just happened as reported in the news - A large corporation requires their delivery drivers to have the money they were owed sent to an account provided by the same corporation which charges the employee for using the account.

Large corporations are bully's because they have the resources the victims do not have.

OVERCHARGING ON SMALL ITEMS

Another item that reflects on corporations taking advantage of customers is to overcharge for small items. Two examples:

1. Seasoning packets, such as Kung Pao chicken, are small packets with maybe a tablespoon of spices. At one time, they cost 59 cents. Today they cost as much as $2. The philosophy is that consumers will not hesitate when so little money is involved so they double or triple the price beyond the normal profit margin. Making such small packets of spices is a very inexpensive cost to the manufacturer so the $2 cost is exorbitant to say the least.
2. Hardware stores fit in this category too. Buy a connector, pipe nipple or even just a small bolt and the price in small quantity is as much as 20 times more than one would pay in bulk.

This is what gave the dollar stores opportunities. They could focus just on the small items and sell for a fraction what the big stores charge. I hope some day Dollar stores will include small hardware and electrical items.

AIRLINE SCAM

I learned another scam the hard way.

Airlines do this frequently. I did not know the financial loss of money and time a cancellation causes until I experienced it. Sun Country cancelled a flight recently leaving us high and dry. We were waiting at the airport to board a plane for a short flight and learned at the last minute that the flight had been cancelled. It was late in the afternoon and we had to be at our destination the next morning. Our tickets had only cost $150. We had to find an alternate flight and there was only one with Delta costing over $600, which landed at midnight making us late for our motel reservation. Cancellation of the room had to be done much earlier so we lost our room and no rooms were left so we had to find another motel. We went to bed after 2 a.m. in the morning.

To make matters worse, we had to request a refund. No automatic refunds are given which means that the airlines typically make added money since many passengers will not spend the time it takes to get a refund. I wonder how many passengers never receive their refund. It took over 1 month to find a person to notify. But frequent follow-ups were still required. We are promised a refund but it took 8 months and numerous emails and telephone calls. Could cancellations be a planned way to turn a flight not full enough to make a profit to a no flight with some profit from those customers who are not able to get a refund or don't have the time? No responsible airline with customer concerns could operate this way but I suspect they all do just as they now all charge for baggage, sometimes more than the flight costs. Who can argue about baggage cost if every airline does it. by the way, I often spend more money on the baggage cost that takes a few hours than I spent for the baggage new.

ONE OF THE BEST

By the way, the corporation that I admire the most is Walmart. They are the most honest large store that I know. They don't price based upon how much they can squeeze out of the consumer but more based upon costs and adding a sensible profit. In most cases they don't look at competition to price an item.

SUMMARY

American corporations in general are taking a great deal of advantage of consumers who cannot afford the legal costs to stand up for their rights.

As you can see from these examples, American business is greedy and shady at times. They need to adopt the American Spirit of fairness to all. They are not just here to make money regardless of the method but to make America a great place to do business where consumers are treated with respect, which they deserve since they are providing the money that enables business to thrive. In my experience a happy customer is a profitable customer.

WHAT CAN BE DONE

Those who are only intent on ripping off the consumers need to be identified and effort made by our government to bring their dishonest techniques to a halt. However, this is not something that laws will fix. As with patriotism, corporations must adopt a different attitude, in this case one of customer fairness.

The media could play a useful part that would help people recognize the problems. The media should be running articles and stories to inform the people in America.

The most effective way to handle greedy corporations is by

customer control. Control the seller instead of having the seller control you. Almost always another seller can be found that is not greedy but looking to sell an excellent product or service and create a happy customer. Let the greedy corporations reap what they sow!

Y.
Waste

America has become a throw away society. We use throw away paper sacks, wrappings, straws, cups, and utensils at most fast-food places. Imagine how many of those are wasted every day.

Surprising to me is that people waste 40% of their food by ordering too much, eating where the food helpings are very large and as the idiom says, their eyes are bigger than their stomachs. What can be done:

- Good food can be taken home and become leftovers.
- Wasted food can go to farms with pigs or to zoos.
- We should have 3 containers to put out each week – garbage, compost material, and recyclables.

Plastics have filled up our waste. We use to sell them to a third world country to recycle them but they have had to cut back after being submerged in plastic waste volume above their capacity to process. Our oceans have island of plastic floating from us and many other countries. What can be done first of all to stop the wasting of plastic in such scenic and useful places as the ocean and secondly to clean up the plastic waste everywhere:

- Solving that problem involves replacing many of the plastic products with paper.

- Disallowing any disposal of plastic in the water ways.
- Using recycled products such as glass often.
- At fast foods separate the plastic from the paper and food. That would enable America to have more control of the plastic.
- I have seen a machine equipped to clean up plastic islands in the ocean. It would probably take thousands of these machines to make a dent in the quantity of plastic but it could be a start.

Composting, the greatest way of rebuilding our planet is ignored by the vast majority. Our waste collectors don't even separate and use the compost material. It boggles the mind to imagine how much compost is wasted. That would recover millions of acres that is infertile.

Waste isn't limited to plastic waste and food. Equipment is often thrown away. Many companies do not fix their products when they fail or replace it with a small part. They throw the complete product or the large assembly in the product away and replace it.

Wasting is a word people see as a natural act but it isn't natural. The earth was created to perpetuate itself and waste was meant to recirculate and help the next generation grow and produce. Whether it is money or food, we have an obligation to not waste which means to throw away. Wasting is not a value issue. Wasting is what the word implies and one must not waste when the item can be useful to others and myself when I am able to use it to say nothing about the denigration of the attractive planet that we have. The word responsibility is a twin word with wasting. One must be responsible not to waste.

Z.
Youth of America

America's future is in the youth of today. What is youth? It has to be the formative years before they assume a full-time job, vote, have families, put forth an effort to make their neighborhoods, cities, states and country better. I might also include joining the United States Service where they have an important adult role.

How important is our youth? As I said above, the future of this country depends upon them. Those of us that have retired are not nearly so responsible or connected as the youth will be. We are in more of a caretaking and reminiscent life but many of us continue to contribute in a major way. Youth however are just starting to see the world in a different life where they are independent and self-supporting. They may have major aspirations or they may just be wondering what they will do.

The youth of today fall into two different categories.

Some are not meeting their responsibility at school because of a lack of interest and effort. They are finding the world is fun in many ways. That may be playing digital games which can captivate your attention for hours if not days at a time. The value is nearly zero to your future. The world of education and part time work is only done as an obligation. Many are even deeply involved in gangs, drugs, alcohol, parties, and sex. Again, the value is nearly zero to their future.

Many of them are benefiting from the education community that is more concerned in making it easy for them than giving them a challenging education. Many parents too are trying to help their youth have fun and be entertained. The parents have been successful and can easily fund a car, vacations, skiing trips and the like. Instead of a little tough love that will make life easier for them down the road, they offer a gravy train.

The other category of youth is the amazing group. I occasionally see an athlete of the year celebrated in an article. Usually, it is because of their exceptional athletic skills and then they go on to describe a young person who is the valedictorian in their class and active in community service. Just reading that list makes me say, "how can anyone be all of that?". Some of the skills, intellect and energy of our youth is awesome and we know that they will make a mark in the world that will change the world. There are many great young people who are disciplined, hard workers and intelligent. What if all young people strive to be healthy, educated, successful and honest? What a country America would be!

What part should the country play in helping the youth achieve tremendous things – inventions, skills, start new companies, become our government, guide our military and protect our country, start families and raise them in a way that will cause them to achieve tremendous things too. Let me list some ways:

- We need to teach discipline, responsibility and civility. Those are character issues in much demand in America.

- Crime should be diminished dramatically. A chapter above deals with that. There should be no safe place in the criminal world for criminals. Our justice system is in great need of becoming one that protects all Americans.

- Education needs to be fixed so that students are safe, challenged and taught lessons that they need in today's world. Today's education leaves so much that is crucial in life out of the curriculum. That should be mandatory and taught yearly. Most parents cannot be relied upon to teach those items because they have not been taught.

- Education should include major training on health because health can extend one's life by 15 years comparing the best to the worst. Nutrition, exercise, addiction issues are major items that every young person should be taught. Our country is in a particularly dangerous place with fast foods and process foods having created a major health problem in our country. They produce food to attract customers instead of provide healthy nutritious products. Taste attracts customers more than nutrition. Sugar, cheese and carbonated drinks are tastier than foods that will help us be healthy, energetic and fit. Selling food and making money is more important to many food producers than having a healthy citizen.

- Education on finances will teach our youth how to save, use their money wisely and enable our youth to be able to enjoy retirement. Retirement requires money and planning which starts right after you turn 21. One is always surprised how fast life goes. Above all they need to learn to live within their means. Nothing is more important.

- Patriotism. Instead of education often trying to educate students on American failures and mistakes, we should teach them about America's successes and the sacrifices that created so many good things in America. We should criticize and denigrate those who want to protest, destroy historical statues, not honor our anthem, and refuse to say the pledge of allegiance. Sounds simple and maybe over the top to some but this is where patriotism begins.

This is a different category of what America could do for the youth but maybe the most important one. Our youth are suffering from a lack of fathers, in some community more than others. Just to give sobering statistic, young criminals who did not grow up with their biological father are almost twice as likely to be idle compared to their male peers from father-present families. Over 90% of felony cases are committed by defendants who grew up on father-absent households. Psychologist Dr. Peter Langman found that most school shooters came from incredibly broken homes. One reference states that 70% of murders are done by boys that had no father. Politifact.com and many other references can be found that detail this.

Fathers are the primary authority to create discipline and responsibilities in boys. This is a task that few women can meet. Women are loving and supporting often times when the boys need just the opposite.

How can that be corrected? Not easy. Lyndon Baines Johnson passed the War on Poverty in the mid 1960's. That gave women the funds to raise children without working. For men it was a bonanza too because they were not so responsible to care for the wife and children. They could do their Romeo act with no requirement to support the wife and child. Lyndon said when he passed it that it would sew up the black vote for decades and it did. The black vote increased over 50% for Democrats and many times 90% or more blacks vote for Democrats.

Removing that welfare is a sure way to lose too many votes to make it practical. Yet what else will work? Perhaps a requirement for all fathers to pay either the government or the mother directly. Leave the existing law alone but make the fathers responsible in some way. That too would be a vote crusher but maybe not so much.

This law illustrates as much as any how laws are passed to buy votes instead of doing what is good for America. Often these same bills are damaging to America as this was incredibly damaging perhaps accounting for over a million murders.

What America becomes in 50 years depends upon what we teach our youth today. I am always baffled by those who turn their children loose on the basis that they can figure it out for themselves not realizing that if you don't teach them, others will and very often they are bad for them and their country.

A Final Word

At this setting, Trump has been elected President and there major changes have and will continue to take place. Some changes, however, will vary from solutions presented in this book. We are hopeful that the changes are ones that will make America better again and we realize the last hundred years has made the job mammoth. America needs new ideas to restore our patriotism, freedom, fairness, and prosperity by everyone. It is the intent of this book to cause citizens to recognize America's problems and offer solutions.

I trust those who are intent on making major changes in our government pledge to improve America. By contrast, many times our leaders seek to reward selected people and ignore the huge problems like debt, the military, Social Security, education and immigration. So often these problems are not thought about as much as immediate wants. For example, adding government jobs is a short-sighted issue that will be rewarded by votes at the cost of the citizens.

The more important issue is the long-term issue of a debt that not only grows fast but requires interest every year. That interest is now over one trillion dollars per year. One trillion dollars, robs us of immediate needs for welfare, social security, Medicare and safety. Government differs from the private world because they don't have to be accountable for profit. They can even borrow trillions with no plan to pay it back but there is a reckoning and that is already costly America a great deal of problems. The debt is even now having a devastating effect on America because it creates more debt and accelerates additional debt.

Two of the problems beyond debt that are of most concern to me are health control and education. These items affect everyone and causes many problems in our society. I believe drastic action must be taken on these two items, as well as many others to make our system more efficient and responsive to today's culture. Ironically, the only way to solve this problem is to turn the private medical system into a socialistic government run system and the socialistic education system into a private system. That sounds illogical but the present systems, socialistic for education and private for medical system, are definitely not working.

Health care is so very overpriced and rife with unnecessary treatments that only extreme measures such as universal care will bring it under control. An insurance-based system that we have is an open checkbook contrary to what it appears. No one is in control of pricing. The system is almost set up for high prices, gouging, performing unnecessary treatment and over medicating plus we have to fund a very large insurance industry that costs $1.5 trillion. That is 1/3 of the health systems total cost. Only government can override the complex system that we now have. Much has to be done to control the unnecessary treatments and medication at prices far beyond other countries. The system that almost every other country uses is universal health care with private/insurance as the customer's option for those who want to pay the price. America must do that as well.

Many have fought universal health care for years but have never created anything else to make our health system competitive in the world. One can always complain and fight an idea but if they have nothing better, the fight is counterproductive.

For education, the existing socialism system is the most expensive in the world and one of the worst of the affluent countries. Until we privatize education, we will continue to waste billions if not trillions while providing a substandard education to our children. We must prepare our children for today's culture and be more responsive to the needs of parents (the customers) to educate their children preparing them for the future. Large cities have poor education in almost every instance. Minneapolis and Milwaukee are notably poor educators especially in the black communities. A recent article in the Washington Times called the Chicago public schools "execrable," which means extremely bad.

This book is intended to make more people aware of the gigantic issues that are costing America freedom, a mammoth debt, threatening the safety of millions of people, and a record setting pace of illegal immigrants invading our borders. Imagine in the last presidential term, enough illegal immigrants are loose in America to populate New York City.

I implore voters to vote on what the person has done rather than on emotional attachment to a Party. Emotion will only bring us to the precipice of democracy and the edge of a cliff is not a good place to live.

We need to be aware not just of those immediate items that affect us but all the items that are bringing America down. We all need to be thinking of our country instead of ourselves because as the country goes, so go we.

About the Author

John Benedict has become an author at a very late time in his life. Having had a career as an engineer turned marketeer, he founded two companies. His work has led to an adventurous life in 5 major cities, attending 16 different churches and living in 14 different houses.

There was little to learn in his schooling about civics but once the 1960's arrived he was gradually captured by the many items happening in government. Through this he became an avid reader about government.

The last 65 years has been a daily study in the revelation of America, the government and the voters. John Benedict has been educated way beyond government 101. Experience beats reading every time.

John Benedict has always been involved in government activities, participating in caucuses, state conventions and volunteer work in his community including sports, and service of every kind in churches. He enjoys Bible Study, dancing at least twice a week, sports, and landscaping, having grown up on a farm.

John and his wife live in Florida. Family is spread out over 6 states and includes children, grandchildren and great-grandchildren.

www.ingramcontent.com/pod-product-compliance
Lightning Source LLC
Chambersburg PA
CBHW020459030426
42337CB00011B/166